AFFIRMpress

Credit: Chris Boyd

Rochelle Siemienowicz is a film critic, journalist, editor and columnist. Her work has been published widely, including in *The Age*, *Kill Your Darlings*, *ScreenHub* and *SBS Movies*. She was for many years the film editor of *The Big Issue*, has worked at the Australian Film Institute | Australian Academy of Cinema & Television Arts, and has a PhD in Australian cinema. Rochelle lives with her partner and son in Melbourne's inner west.

fallen

rochelle siemienowicz

*a memoir about sex, religion
and marrying too young*

Published by Affirm Press in 2015
28 Thistlethwaite Street, South Melbourne, VIC 3205.
www.affirmpress.com.au

National Library of Australia Cataloguing-in-Publication entry available
for this title at www.nla.gov.au
Title: Fallen: a memoir about sex, religion and marrying too young/
Rochelle Siemienowicz, author.
ISBN: 9781922213655 (paperback)

Cover design by Josh Durham/Design by Committee
Typeset in 11.5/16 Granjon by J&M Typesetting
Proudly printed in Australia by Griffin Press

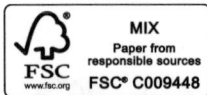

FSC
www.fsc.org

MIX
Paper from
responsible sources
FSC® C009448

The paper this book is printed on is certified against the Forest Stewardship
Council® Standards. Griffin Press holds FSC chain of custody certification
SGS-COC-005088. FSC promotes environmentally responsible, socially beneficial
and economically viable management of the world's forests.

Australian Government

Australia Council for the Arts

This project has been assisted by the Australian Government through
the Australia Council, its arts funding and advisory body.

For Vanessa, who said,
'I'll tell you everything.' Love eternally.

And to all those who helped me live this story,
and tell this story, I thank you. You are golden and
I will never forget what I owe.

Call me Eve.

Of course it's not my real name. My good Christian parents would have considered it a curse to give their baby girl the name of that original sinner, the woman who brought pain and evil into the world when she gave in to temptation. But it's the name I call myself when I think back to that time when I was a young wife — so very young, so very hungry — and I picked the fruit and ate and drank until I was drunk with freedom and covered in juice and guilt.

But not regret.

Because when I tell this story — and it is a story, with parts made up and fragments rearranged like a dream half remembered now that twenty years have passed — I see that my world exists because of it. Like the first woman in the oldest story, I said 'yes' instead of 'no', and there was never any question of turning back.

Prologue

The lights are on in the room next door and I can hear prayers. My father leads them, answered by murmurs of assent and 'Amen' from the group. The piano starts up; that will be my mother, straight-backed and tense, adding tinkling flourishes as they sing hymns. From my bed I watch the golden strip of light that glows through the crack under my door. I imagine that I can see the prayers wafting in like incense to protect me and send me to sleep in Jesus' arms.

But it's not Jesus I want as my hands find their way under my blue cotton nightie. I'm only nine but already I love the feeling of fingers on my skin, in the places I know I shouldn't touch. I imagine what it will be like one day, when I've found my husband, and he will be the one to take me, every night, and make me breathless and hot the way I make myself. I'm not exactly sure how this will work – or even what he'll look like without his clothes on. But I know I want it and I know we'll be bound together forever, our bodies 'made one flesh in the sight of God', the way my father says it when he's marrying a couple and telling them to love one another as Christ loved the Church.

I don't dream of being a bride. I don't care about the dress or the ring or the babies that are allowed no less than ten months after the wedding. I just want that man, the one I imagine in the dark, because he'll know me and want me and make me clean again. He'll take me to that place where I feel like I'm flying and all the sunbursts come together behind my eyes in one shuddering golden sigh.

I won't be a dirty girl then. I'll be his wife.

I

MELBOURNE, 1992

I'm standing in my undies and bra. Mum's kneeling at my feet, the metal edge of a tape measure pressed hard against my belly button. She's measuring the length of me from my waist to the floor. It doesn't look like very much when she moves the tape away and compares it against the crunchy paper dressmaker's pattern that's spread on the carpet of her bedroom.

We're making my wedding dress. I'm twenty years old.

'I love it,' I say, as I pick up the soft, heavy piece of white satin, five rippling metres of it bought from Lincraft at Chadstone.

'Don't mess it up,' she says, seeing me drape the material around my body, pulling it tight over my hips.

I'm smiling at myself in the winged mirror of her dressing table. 'It's exactly the right colour.' The ice-white lights up my face, making me look pink and healthy instead of yellow and sick, the way the ivory did.

But Mum frowns. 'Hmm.'

'You don't like it?'

'It's very nice,' she says primly. 'Isaac should be pleased when he sees you walk down the aisle.' She pulls the fabric away from me and starts to fold it neatly.

'But?'

'It's just that I always imagined this would mean something,' she says. 'The whiteness of it.'

'Are you serious, Mum?'

'White is for virgins,' she says with her back to me, looking for her pearl-headed pins in the sewing basket.

'And what am I, a dirty whore who's slept with two men before I get married? So I don't deserve to wear white?' Goosebumps prickle along my arms. I wrap my nubby bathrobe around me, pulling the sash tight into an angry knot at my waist. 'I can't believe we're having this conversation. It's the *nineties*.'

'Darling, don't speak so crassly. I'd never call you a … a prostitute. It's just that when you were a little girl, I dreamt of getting you ready for your big day. And I always thought the wedding night would be … special.'

I watch her through the mirror's right panel as she wipes away a tear. She makes a nick in the white satin with her black metal sewing shears, then rips the fabric all the way down with her hands – a long, tidy slice that will become the fishtail flounce at the bottom.

I chose this design because I want to look like a thirties black-and-white movie star, snaky hips and satin rippling in a pale wave when I walk. The neck, hem and sleeves will be covered in delicate ecru feathers, which tickle my nose now as I pull a lengthy string of them out of the paper bag, wrapping them round my neck like a feather boa.

I want to be the kind of smart-talking, sassy bride who looks as though she's lived a little; the kind of bride who's chosen her husband in the tradition of all great Hollywood romantic comedies, to be her wise-cracking playmate. A best friend and lover in one unconventional package.

Yes, that's Isaac. I wish I could kiss him right now and relay this astonishing conversation I'm having with my mother. But he's at uni, in a lecture, or studying in the halls of residence where he lives. Actually, he's probably playing with his Game Boy, or strumming his guitar and making up a song that he'll play for me later while I lie on his unmade single bed, watching his fingers and his mouth, and wanting them on me. Which they will be, when the song ends and he comes to lie down with me, his long, lean body pressed against mine, and his sleepy golden eyes laughing at me behind his round John Lennon glasses. Laughing because my hunger for him is so naked and undisguised. He's not used to being so desired.

We're going to be married in mid-semester break.

I don't want to look like a cream puff or a taffeta soufflé, and I certainly don't need to look like a virgin. But at the same time I hope that some of the wedding guests, the more conservative ones who don't know me so well, might still think I deserve my white dress.

I pray each night before I go to sleep, imagining that God understands and forgives my lapses, especially now I'm engaged.

'I guess you're disappointed we can't hang a blood-smeared sheet up in front of the guests after I've been deflowered,' I say. 'Like the Jews used to do.'

Mum doesn't answer, but keeps cutting, tight-lipped and sniffing back the tears – histrionically, I think.

Virginity. The ways in which boys are free – or excused – and girls are not; the ways in which tribes keep themselves pure and enclosed, with property ownership secured through female chastity. I've been learning about this in second-year sociology at the brown-brick, second-tier university where I'm discovering that I'm a freak, from a freakish religion. Other people live without these rules and all this guilt, and they haven't dissolved into moral decay, the way I'd imagined a godless life might be. They can be kind and honest and even modest; they can care about the state of the world and their fellow human beings, even if they believe we evolved from apes.

'Mum,' I say firmly, 'you were a virgin when you got married, which is great. That was the sixties. But the two men I've slept with, I fully intended to marry. So I don't think I'm cheating by wearing white.'

'I know,' she says, resigned, but she's not going to give me the approval I want.

'You agreed that ivory washes me out, so don't make me feel bad for choosing proper white.'

I'm playing with my hair now, wondering if I should pile it up or leave it loose on the day. I hardly care. I want to look beautiful, but really I just want the wedding to be over and done with so I can get to the part where Isaac and I are living on our own.

'Nobody said you *couldn't* wear white.' Mum brushes another tear away, looking wounded. 'I'm making the dress for you, aren't I?' She holds some material up to the light, determining the grain of the fabric, before laying it down with the pattern on top.

She's made so many clothes for me, starting when I was a tiny girl in New Guinea and Fiji. There were sunsuits and frilly hats, and matching versions in blue for my younger brother Aiden; people thought we were twins when we were toddlers. Mum even sewed bathers for me, in red and white checked gingham that sagged and faded fast in the chlorine of our above-ground swimming pool. But mostly the clothes were fabulous, almost perfect, and I thought she was a miracle worker.

She kept on making dresses for me when I was a teenager in Perth and being well dressed meant so much. I'd sketch an outfit or tear a picture from a magazine – Audrey Hepburn was my idol – and she'd stay up late into the night, sewing so I could wear the new dress to church on Sabbath, or to the Friday night Youth Fellowship that Seventh-day Adventist teenagers used as a fashion parade. We were supposed to sing hymns and pray, and listen to stories of missionaries returned from the Pacific and the miracles they'd witnessed with the natives – but we were mainly looking at each other.

Sometimes the returned missionary was my father, the Minister, and I wanted to die of embarrassment as he stood at the front of the church, stepping away from the pulpit with a handheld microphone because this was Friday night, not Sabbath, and the youth deserved 'a more casual approach'. Though he could never quite do casual, my dad, I had to admit I was proud of him. He was so tall and poised in his suit and tie, not a dark hair out of place on his handsome head. I'd find myself listening with eagerness to his familiar stories of dolphins saving shipwrecked sailors who'd prayed in desperation; or miraculous healings in mountaintop villages where no doctor could tread; or persecutions in China and Russia, where owning a Bible could result in imprisonment.

Dad would ask us if we'd be ready to give up our lives for our faith. Or would we, like Peter the Apostle, deny Jesus three times before the cock crowed?

My religious fervour waxed and waned, but I was always most interested in seeing my friends and flirting with the boys, who were all a little afraid of my father. And I loved dressing up in the new clothes that Mum would lay on my bed like magic, ironed and finished in an overnight flurry.

I loved the way she wanted me to be beautiful. She praised my breasts when they eventually came in so much larger than hers. She told me my legs were lovely. She fitted my skirts perfectly around my little waist, calling me her Barbie doll, and joked that she'd 'make it as tight as we can while you can still breathe'.

Now, standing in front of her on a cold Melbourne winter's day, as she makes my wedding dress, I know I've disappointed her. I didn't understand that it was all for show; it was the bait to catch the fish – the husband who would keep me safe. And even though I've found the husband, I've spoilt it all because I rushed.

'You're making me feel really bad,' I tell her. 'I can't believe this.'

'I'm sorry, darling.' Mum sniffs again. 'I just wish you'd waited, that's all. I'm grieving for the dream I had of my daughter's wedding. Am I allowed to do that?'

And there she is, honest and monstrous all at once – a little girl and an old matriarch together in the one still-pretty package. She's only forty-four.

I'm never sure where I stand with Mum. I wobble on unstable ground, dodging weapons that seem unearthed from a Victorian arsenal. Sometimes she's so modern; I enjoy her when she's like that, light and happy and silly. At those times her conversation is streaked with disarming dashes of rebellious, perceptive wit and a shocking honesty combined with self-deception.

We're alike in so many ways.

'Your mum is hardcore,' my girlfriends used to say as they observed her, one of the strictest Seventh-day Adventist mothers, lighting candles on Friday night and confiscating *Dolly*. She'd insist on us keeping my bedroom door open while we chatted – 'in case you get up to mischief' – naughtiness of a kind she would never specify. 'Does she think we're lesbians?' my best friend Esther would ask with a giggle, as she pushed the door until it was open just enough to follow the rules.

'Your mum is scary,' my teenage boyfriend Marcus would whisper in my ear as she walked out of the room, giving him a glance that told him to keep his hands off me. 'She makes me feel like I'm always disappointing her.' He'd nuzzle into my neck, his hands creeping under my t-shirt, before she returned. 'It's like she can read my mind and knows I'm bad.'

I knew exactly what he meant.

But then she'd be in the backyard on a Sunday afternoon, wearing very short shorts and wielding a shovel, muscles defined in her thin brown arms while she dug holes in the sandy soil for bottlebrush shrubs; she was 'going native', as every sensible West Australian gardener did in the eighties.

She'd smile and wave back at us, eyes masked by big Jackie O sunglasses. And then Claudia, my second-best friend, whose house was just down the road and who practically lived at my place after school, would say, 'Your mum looks kind of hot, you know?' And I had to admit she did.

She was the mother most likely to talk about tampons and periods and bras. My girlfriends felt comfortable being women with her. And strict as she was, she was also the mother who gave my brother and me a matter-of-fact sex education when we were just five and three. She sat us down, two little peas in the pod of the big, round rattan chair on our porch in Kavieng, New Ireland, where the tip of New Guinea nearly kisses the equator. Aiden and I were covered in bandaids and mosquito bites, wearing underpants and singlets in the steamy heat. Mum knelt beside us, showing us a colourful book filled with medical illustrations of the uterus, vagina and penis. She told us calmly and without shame about how the husband put his penis into the wife's vagina and that was how you made a baby.

'It's beautiful,' she said, 'the way God made us.'

Yet I never saw her, or another grown-up person, naked. Returned from the mission fields and back in Perth, at age eleven I was confused by the appearance of dark, spindly hairs on my own body. I tried to wash them off in the shower, then pinched them with my fingernails, wincing at the pain and realising with revulsion that they were attached. What were they for?

I had to ask Esther behind the church toilets on Sabbath. We'd both got our first pair of kitten heels that year – white Candy court shoes. We wobbled as we tiptoed over the grass, trying to avoid sinking the sharp points into the soil.

'Sit down here,' said Esther, gesturing to the concrete kerb and pulling a cherry-red lip gloss out of her gold Glomesh handbag. 'Want some?' she asked, handing it over to me. I hesitated: I was only supposed to wear clear lip gloss and clear nail polish. 'So the hair thing,' she said. 'What are you worried about?'

'Is it … normal?' I whispered.

She nodded.

'But it's disgusting!'

'You're an idiot,' she said gently, her hand on my wrist. 'Haven't you ever seen your parents? Hasn't your mum told you about … stuff?'

'Not that bit. What else should I know?'

'Don't worry.' Esther snapped her purse shut and leant back against the red-brick wall. Her blonde hair, moussed up into the kind of curly bob Madonna wore, was sticking to the bricks like velcro. 'I'll tell you everything.'

~

'Don't mind me,' Mum says, blowing her nose on a white linen hankie, the kind with pink rosebuds embroidered on the corners. She always keeps one tucked into her bra strap while she works, wary of tears or hay fever. 'I'm just being silly.'

She kneels on the floor, where the paper has been carefully pinned to the satin in a complicated jigsaw – sleeves next to skirt, upside down, like bones disassembled from a body. She cuts into it boldly.

'We need to get this wedding dress finished,' she says. 'There's not much time left.'

2

PERTH, 1996

Four years after my Melbourne wedding, I've touched down in Perth for a holiday. Safe landings make me euphoric; I'm convinced every plane will crash, and I feel like I've cheated death when Esther and Claudia pick me up at the airport.

The night air, stinking of kerosene, is warm and dense as we walk from the terminal to the car park. The girls, my old bridesmaids, look faded and summery, though it's only December. I've forgotten how early the heat comes here; my black velvet jeans, so right for Melbourne, are hot and heavy.

'So strokeable,' says Esther, reaching down to caress the fabric as we walk arm in arm.

I lean in to her and wonder if this is why I'm drawn to feathers and fur, velvet and suede – because I like to be touched.

'Aren't you sweltering?' Claudia asks. She walks a little apart, pulling my big black suitcase behind her, heaving it up onto the kerb with a sigh. 'How much stuff did you bring, anyway?'

'She's here for a few weeks,' says Esther. 'She needs a *lot* of clothes.'

'I know, but it's like lead!' Claudia smiles at me and shakes her head, making it clear that it's Esther she's cross with, for leaving her with the heavy lifting.

'Sorry, I brought lots of books too,' I say, making Claudia groan again.

These girls, my oldest friends and still my closest, are tired and edgy. University exams have just finished and they've been living in a house together for a year. I can feel the tension of too-familiar friends sharing everything, of their frayed generosity and strained civility, the money owing and the favours being counted and recounted, the petty housework arguments. I've heard both sides in long midnight phone calls. Esther rings in anger and frustration; Claudia sobs out her words. I listen, sitting by the kitchen window of my Oakleigh flat, looking at the moon above the concrete car park, winding the phone cord around and around my wrist as I struggle to follow the thread of who said what and who's at fault. And always, Isaac is calling out to me from the bedroom, annoyed at being woken up.

Now Esther and Claudia compete for my attention as they lift my suitcase into the boot and usher me to the front passenger seat as if I'm visiting royalty. Words spill out. They're talking on top of each other, louder and louder, voices swooping in to intersect and contradict stories about the party they went to last night and the trouble they had getting a ride back. Then they're bickering and I can't be bothered keeping up.

I wish they could feel as good about each other as I feel about them both right now.

I wind down the window and breathe in fumes that smell like adventure and escape, but also like coming home. When was the last time all three of us were together? Was it four years ago when we slept on mattresses in my parents' lounge room, the night before my wedding, whispering into the early hours?

No, actually it was two years ago when I came to Perth for Easter and we went camping in Margaret River, getting our car bogged on a muddy back road and hitchhiking into town in the dark for help. 'You could have been killed, you stupid girls,' said Isaac when I told him from a phone booth. He wasn't happy that I'd left him home alone to be with my friends. He'd been invited, of course, but said he was allergic to camping and wanted the house to himself anyway.

Driving fast down a freeway that's so vividly blank, I feel alive. White lines stretching out forever, pointing to infinity. Esther puts her foot to the accelerator and speeds, careless about limits as always, and it feels like there's nothing to catch us, nothing to stop us from flying up joyfully into the clear dark skies.

But we speak of death.

'Simon's funeral was yesterday,' Esther says, suddenly solemn as she jerks to a stop at a red light intersection near an industrial site. Giant silos pump clouds of pale waste, blotting out the stars. I shut the window so I can hear her better. 'Claudia went to "pay her respects".' Esther looks over at Claudia in the back seat, and as she accelerates I wish she'd keep her eyes on the road. 'I don't know why you bothered,' she adds. 'You didn't even *like* him.'

'I started Grade One with him,' says Claudia obstinately. 'We were both kept down a year. It was horrible being older than everyone else, getting boobs first – well, I did, and he was shaving. But we still couldn't keep up.' She pauses. 'He knew what it was like to be bad at school.'

Esther and I smile at her. She's always telling us how stupid she is; how much smarter we are. But we know she's brilliant. Literal and innocent, like her black hair and white skin and her red, red lips. Snow White with her practical streak.

'I would have gone to the funeral if I'd been here,' I say. 'I've been thinking about Simon all week, ever since Mum rang me up to tell me the news. I knew he was sick. Really sick.'

'Who told your mum?' asks Claudia. 'Isn't she still in the Solomon Islands?'

'The great Seventh-day Adventist grapevine, I guess. They probably know what we're doing right at this minute.'

'Yuck, it's so creepy,' says Esther. 'Such a cult. Can you believe we were brought up thinking we were going to live through the end of the world?' She crunches vehemently into third gear. 'That's child abuse, you know.'

'Well, how did you find out about Simon?' I ask.

'Same way. Claudia's grandma goes to church with his mum.'

'There's no escape,' I say. 'It's "Hotel California", Sev style.'

I do find it unnerving how the gossip travels, but I hate it when Esther calls the Church a cult, mainly because my parents have lectured me so often about what defines a cult and how they don't live in one.

'We have perfectly sane, though uniquely biblical, Protestant beliefs,' my father tells people. He loves to be asked questions that allow him to defend his faith. He has to be stopped – which I do rudely, while he demurs patiently – or he'll go on for hours, stacking up scriptural and historical evidence, together with his own convictions.

The truth is I'm glad of the grapevine sometimes, its tendrils reaching out to curl around me with news that I care about, even now I've 'left the flock'. I hadn't seen Simon in years, but I wish I'd been here to say goodbye to a fellow traveller, no matter how tenuous our connection. I'm sure I would have cried at his grave, remembering him when he was a dark, sweet child, sitting across from me in Grade Five and sweating over his spelling test; and later, when he was a brooding seventeen-year-old, silently watching me kiss his best friend, Marcus, before the two of them drove away from church, with me resentfully left behind.

'Another one bites the dust,' Claudia says, suddenly matter-of-fact. 'Who's next?' She scans the car, leaning forward from the back seat like a grim reaper, and we laugh nervously.

Out of our high school graduating class of thirty, two have died of leukaemia. There was another kid too, from a grade below us. Was there something in the water? Or maybe it was the power lines that crisscrossed our little brick school up there on the hill overlooking the beautiful Bickley Valley, right next door to the Sanitarium Health Food factory with its sweet, yeasty Weet-Bix fumes. We travelled there in buses every day from all across the city, to learn and worship among the orange groves, the birds and that grain-flavoured fresh air. Was there something else in the air?

Or was there something wrong with the vegetarian health food our mothers served up to us in our lunchboxes? Nutmeat sandwiches on wholegrain bread, fresh fruit, and carefully wrapped slices of carrot and walnut cake sweetened with honey. But what could be wrong with that?

We were always hearing that Adventists lived longer than

other people; that no smoking, no drinking, no meat and no sex before marriage made for long lives. We'd joke that our lives just seemed longer from boredom and frustration – and the fact that Sabbath afternoons wore into tedious eternity with no play, no work and no fun until sundown. But we enjoyed the statistics and looked forward to living long lives, so these young deaths stung badly.

'I *did* want to cry about Simon,' admits Esther, who has a strong and illogical sense of social propriety. 'But I kept putting it off until after exams and now I mightn't be able to.' She pauses, and I know she's testing her emotions as if taking her temperature. 'Claudia cried buckets, though. Didn't you?' She keeps her eyes on the road this time, her tone faintly mocking.

Claudia seems embarrassed. I can imagine the great gushing tears and sobs, the wine-hazy crying she does whenever she's confronted with mortality. It's understandable – her parents died in a car crash when she was little. She hates to think of her own limited lifespan. She applies sunscreen and swallows vitamins with zeal.

I change the subject from tears to gossip. 'Who was at the funeral?'

Esther and Claudia look at each other.

'Marcus,' Esther says.

I open my eyes wide and remind myself to breathe.

Claudia is scornful. 'He was his usual self. He cried and made a speech, mostly about himself – and what a bright star he was in Simon's orbit. What a dickhead.'

'He flew over from Sydney?' I ask, finding it hard to imagine him organising himself at short notice.

'I guess so. Didn't talk to him. Why should I?'

'You could have put yourself out for some information,' I suggest.

'I didn't think you'd want it,' says Claudia. 'He treated you like shit.'

I love that she's still pissed off on my behalf.

Esther waves away Claudia's aggression with one lazy hand, as if it's a mildly bad smell that's floated in through the window. She doesn't have the attention span for grudges or for hating ex-boyfriends, and she's hungry for drama.

'Are you going to ring him?' she asks me. 'He might still be in Perth.'

'I haven't spoken to him in five years ...'

She looks mischievous. 'Go on. You should.'

'Don't even think about it,' says Claudia.

I look out the window at these flat familiar streets and wonder if it's safe now. I have a husband I love back in Melbourne, where I live a world away from Marcus' ridiculous charm and his reputedly sordid Sydney life. He poses no threat, I think.

'What's he even doing now?' asks Esther.

'Drugs, probably,' says Claudia. 'Remember that girl he brought to church when he was visiting a few years ago for Easter Big Camp? That really skinny one who looked like a heroin addict?'

'Didn't someone see a gun at his place in Sydney?' says Esther with relish. 'I heard that somewhere.'

'So skanky,' says Claudia.

'But kind of intriguing.' Esther smiles over at me.

She's right. I'm a little bit curious to investigate that grimy glamour. I want to know what kind of fate I've escaped. I want to congratulate myself on the dead wood I've shed. It feels as if my nose is suddenly pressed up tight against the rear window with its fast-receding landscape. I want to know.

~⊙

Marcus, Marcus, love of my life. Brown-skinned and thin as a whippet, with merry dark eyes and a wide white smile that cracked open his face when he laughed – which was often, because Marcus never stopped talking and laughing. Love of my life – that was the role I cast him in when I 'gave it all up' at seventeen, so solemn and serious and sure that I'd never be with another man.

Are there still girls who think this way, or boys who promise marriage in their teens? Probably in other religious enclaves where sex is forbidden before the honeymoon and young couples grapple with the sweet, sticky compromises this entails. The aching, longing, loaded hours of Saturday nights in cars, or kissing in the back row of the cinema with the stench of stale popcorn and the bloat from giant buckets of fizzy drink.

It sounds so fifties, so American; it makes me think of twinsets, and pearls and prom nights and getting to second base against a classic rock'n'roll soundtrack. Except for us it was the late eighties and romantic ballads dripped from the radio as we drove the dry West Australian highways from rollerskating rink to bowling alley to basketball practice, pulling in at McDonald's to stuff our faces guiltily with burgers – our gateway drug to eating meat – before finding somewhere to park and neck.

Then we'd work out those compromises, deal by deal, date by date, promise by promise, until we were naked and breathless, but still 'waiting'.

'We should stop,' I'd say, wriggling out from beneath Marcus on the squeaky back seat of his mother's old car, where his cock was resting, damp on my thigh, precariously close to slipping inside me and puncturing my precious hymen.

'Should we?' He'd sigh. 'I guess we should. Can't you just … suck me, then?'

'Of course, come here.' I'd take him in my mouth with a smile, watching him above me, because I loved him, because I liked the power I had over him when he came, and because he'd soon do the same for me.

We did the best we could – three years of 'everything else' – until at seventeen we guiltily stole the prize and vowed to earn it later.

It was a Sabbath afternoon. Marcus and I washed the lunch dishes while my mother napped in the other room, full of the heavy meal with its three courses, prepared on Friday afternoon to avoid work on the holy day itself. Dad was away on a country preaching trip that weekend, and things always felt less formal then, as if we could all breathe out and stretch the rules a little bit.

As I wiped the glasses and plates that Marcus slopped ineptly on the draining board, I looked at him and loved him with that familiar kick in my gut. He was mine and I wanted to be his, without reservation.

I wrapped my arms around his waist from behind, and whispered into his warm neck. 'Let's do it today. All the way.'

'Where did that come from?' he asked, turning around with a confused grin, pulling me in for a kiss and wiping his wet, soapy hands on my skirt.

I pushed him away and threw him a tea towel. 'I've just decided. It's time. When Mum goes out later to drop Aiden at choir practice, we'll have the house to ourselves for half an hour.'

After we watched the car leave the driveway and head along the street, we got down to business, right in front of the curtained lounge-room window. We wouldn't be caught out in the bedroom down the back of the house – no way.

'Are you sure? Are you *really* ready?' Marcus asked as he unwrapped the single condom that lived hopefully in his wallet. I nodded and he knelt between my legs for that quick private ceremony we'd been building up to for three years, since we'd first kissed in the draughty locker room in Grade Nine. 'You know what this means,' he said, poised above me.

I felt as if we were pricking fingers to bind us in blood forever.

'I do,' I said.

'Till death do us part?' he asked dramatically. Marcus was prone to drama. He saw himself always at the centre of an exciting story where truth was less important than aesthetics – it was part of why I loved him. But his dark eyes were serious now. I wanted to laugh out of habit, to break the tension, but I stopped myself. This was a deed we could never retract or erase from the story of us.

'Just do it. We don't have very long.' I clutched his arse and brought him to the brink of penetration. My thick woollen skirt was up around my waist, my legs winter-pale against his light-brown African skin. I kissed his neck, burying my nose in him and breathing in the scent that was so sweet to me even when he tried to cover it up with too much Brut.

Then I felt him breaking in – a new pain, sharp and stabbing. Then it was gone, and in its place a sense of fullness and completeness, almost familiar, as if we'd been doing this for years.

He pulled his head back so I could see his face, smiling at me, pure joy and love, but also as though he was going to burst. I lay there quite still, absorbed by the look of him, the feel of this new thing inside me. 'Aren't you going to come?' he asked, knowing what it was like to make me climax from years of practice with his fingers and his mouth, but never like this. 'I want you to. I can hold on.'

'I don't want to this time,' I said wonderingly, and he looked surprised – I was usually so greedy. 'I just want to be here. It's enough.'

'Whatever you want,' he said, shutting his eyes and losing himself in his own experience, while I observed from a little distance, preserving the memory, amazed at the beauty of it, the beauty of him, and the fact that what we were doing had eternal significance.

How could this be wrong? I'd never felt so sure of anything. The public wedding could wait – we'd decided we would announce our engagement at my eighteenth birthday and get married at twenty-one. Surely this wasn't a real sin. And if it *was*, we'd ask for forgiveness. Later.

We're turning the corner into Esther's driveway. Her big old house, two streets back from the Swan River, is the family home I never had.

My missionary parents don't stay in any house longer than a year or two. 'Twenty-two houses in thirty years of marriage,' says Mum, wearily but proudly, whenever people ask her about the flattened and faded cardboard moving boxes brought out of the shed yet again because Dad has been 'called' – by the Holy Spirit, he implies, but really it's just a job offer – to minister to another flock in another part of the world.

During my childhood we made daring leaps to New Guinea and Fiji – and later, after I'd left home, they went to the Solomon Islands – places where the people were poor and hungry for hope. These big moves were for the Lord's work; always there was the conviction that Dad was the right man for the right place. The 'still small voice' of God, filtered through his prayerful conscience, told him where he must go. And we would follow.

Then there were moves between Australian cities – Newcastle, Melbourne, Perth, Adelaide, Brisbane – or sometimes within a city, because Dad had decided to build another house, or sell another house, or merely move to a different suburb. This was the case when we lived here in Perth – first when I was in Grades Five and Six, and then later when we came back from Port Moresby for me to do the last five years of high school – Dad gritting his teeth and staying in one job to give his teenagers some stability. In those years we lived in six houses, and a couple of the moves were mere streets away.

It was exhausting and destabilising, this setting up home and dismantling it before the newly planted trees were grown or the neighbours properly met. Mum complained about the fifteen heavy boxes of theological textbooks that had to be packed and carted. But there was a part of her that loved abandoning one set of problems for a fresh set in a new location. My brother and I moaned a little about changing schools, leaving pets and saying goodbye to friends, especially as we grew older. But mostly we accepted it, because this was the way our world worked and God was leading.

So Esther's is a kind of home for me: a place to come back to, a place where my feet touch the grass, the same grass, year after year. I look up at the house, with its bedroom lights all ablaze. I remember the first time I came here, when I was nine and Esther brought me home for lunch after befriending me at church. I hadn't been able to stop staring at her that day, as she sang lustily and loudly with the hymn book held up high in front of her. She glanced over at me, her bright blue eyes full of life. I saw that she had scandalous pierced ears, which made me wonder if she was a new convert, not yet au fait with the Church's stance on jewellery. But she'd sat quite still and, with rapt attention, listened to my father preach from the pulpit, smiling along when he told a joke, and frowning with empathy as he spoke of the cross and the pain Christ suffered when the nails were bashed in. She kept her eyes tightly shut during prayers, while my own were roaming the audience for detail.

I wanted more of her worldly nine-year-old glamour; I longed to have my own virgin ears pierced. And as we sat on the grass in her garden after lunch (our parents still inside around the ruins of the Sabbath banquet) we painted our fingernails – me for the first time, venturing only to pearlescent pink. I looked at Esther's collection of tiny bottles lined up on the pavement next to the flowering Geraldton wax bush – lolly pink, gothic purple, aqua blue. They made a wicked eighties rainbow that I wanted to follow.

Fifteen years later, the garden has grown lush and wild and looks like it might eat us alive. Esther's parents are in Hong Kong for a year, where her businessman father has a short-term contract, so the trees, grass and vines are unleashed by carelessness, surviving on bore water and fading traces of fertiliser. The sexy black fingers of man-sized ferns reach out in the night, across the front door, as I struggle past with my suitcase. I feel a mosquito's nose stinging its way into my cheek, and I shiver, almost with pleasure, because this means it's hot enough for mosquitoes. I've come home to summer.

~⦿

Claudia's gone to bed.

'She just sleeps and sleeps!' says Esther with disdain. She doesn't need much sleep; she's strong and proud and sucks the life right out of the day and night as if she's scared she'll miss something. She often pushes me to stay awake until dawn, just for the kick of it.

We're sitting on the lounge-room carpet in a seventies conversation pit, with a smoked-glass coffee table and fawn-coloured velveteen couch. There's an enormous dried floral arrangement of native flowers and pieces of bark in the corner, rising out of lumpish homemade pottery. Orange and brown, it's covered in dust and surely hasn't been touched since 1978.

Esther's eyes burn brightly – too brightly – as she sips her white wine. She's been popping dexamphetamines to get through exams. They might have done her some good if they'd been given to her when she was an inattentive child, long before ADD diagnoses were being made, but now it's all just speed to her.

'I've been awake for days,' she says intensely, 'and I don't think I'm going to sleep tonight either.' She takes my hand, her lovely, pointy fingers twining between mine, and smiles.

It's been six months since we've seen each other – her last visit to Melbourne came in the middle of winter during mid-semester break. We'd shivered in our fake furs, numb fingers clutching mugs of hot chocolate at a cafe in Brunswick Street, and planned this summer holiday. 'We *need* it,' Esther had insisted. 'A long time together, not just a week. For our relationship.' She spoke seriously, as if we were in a marriage. Inspired by Anne and Diana in *Anne of Green Gables*, we'd sworn 'eternal love' and best-friendship on her tenth birthday, and proceeded with high seriousness as each anniversary passed. There was never any question that as old ladies, we'd still be best friends.

So much of our friendship is conducted by distance now. When school finished, I moved to Melbourne with my family, while Esther spent two years in Europe, delaying university. She began as a missionary in the newly opened wilds of Eastern Europe, where the former communists now wanted Jesus, but she quickly lost her faith. After that, she stayed to party in England. Between us there have been so many crunchy blue airmail letters, and so many expensive, late-night telephone calls. But there's no substitute for this, sitting arm to arm, warm skin touching.

'You smell so good,' I say, sniffing the jasmine scent of her hair.

Our backs are against the couch, our heads steepled together, my dark one and her golden one. We used to sleep that way in church, or on the bus to school in the early winter mornings, when the warm air crept up our skirts and the humming of the engine made conversation difficult. The smell of our shampoos and Impulse deodorant mists would mingle in an overpowering chemical fug.

Esther's playing with my wedding ring now. Such a plain, thin vein of gold on my finger. I love it deeply, this ordinary treasure, even though I'm so careless with it, taking it off to cook or do the dishes, and forgetting to put it back on for days. But this ring is the piece of shiny magic that makes me who I am, reminding me of my story and the safe and happy ending that follows me, no matter where I stray.

'How's Isaac?' Esther asks.

It still feels strange to me that she hardly knows my husband. These two people veer off from me in different directions, their pull equal and opposite.

'Honestly? I'm glad to be away from him for a while.' I picture Isaac bent over his keyboard, hour after hour, raising his head occasionally but never losing the visionary fervour that comes when he's writing code. I've longed for him to focus on me like that, the way he did when we first met, before I was a game played out and won: a conquered world with no more levels to complete.

'Poor Isaac,' Esther says, without feeling.

'He'll play the martyr, but he'll be happy. Pizza, videos and sleeping in. Living in a mess. Geek heaven. At least for the first few days before he misses me, and it's only two weeks till he's here.'

'Mm.' She stretches out on the shag pile and narrows her eyes. 'Two whole weeks to ourselves. But you've got that conference to go to, and then your *lover* coming next week.' She says the word with deliberate self-consciousness, as though it's faintly ridiculous for me to have a lover at twenty-four.

I laugh. 'I almost wish my *lover* wasn't coming so we could be on our own. I can see Jay anytime in Melbourne.'

'Does Isaac mind about Jay coming to stay?'

'I asked, of course, and he said it was up to me.'

'And if he'd said no?'

'I would've accepted it. He *is* my husband.'

'Well, forgive me if I don't know all the rules!' Esther turns over on her belly, resting on her elbows with her bright face in her hands. 'So what's he like?'

'He's alright.'

We giggle. What kind of an answer is that? I try to imagine what Esther will make of Jay. I'm not sure she'll like him, or that she'll be able to see what I see in him.

'He can be pompous and annoying,' I warn. 'He's a professional *critic*.'

'An art *cricket*!' she says in a bad Cockney accent. 'Rubbing his little legs together and making a buzzy, self-important noise.'

We smile at each other, then start laughing, working ourselves up into hysteria that far outweighs the joke. We're sucking in the air between us until we're dizzy with the sight of each other's faces. I remember how many times we've been here before, drunk on each other.

Finally I'm calm enough to defend Jay. 'He pays attention – real attention. And he takes me seriously.'

'He takes your *body* seriously. Sounds like you've been doing nothing but fucking since you met him.'

'No, honestly. Mind and body.'

Esther raises an eyebrow. 'How serious are you?' she asks.

I like it that she's not timid with me – but I hate the question. Isaac's been pushing it under the door at me throughout the months since I met Jay, though he won't ask me outright. How serious am I about this latest interloper, this man I write and talk to every day, this man whose bed I run to in the afternoons when I'm meant to be writing a PhD thesis and Isaac is at work?

'I've had feelings of ... *tenderness*,' I say.

Her grin turns into a wince. 'You're not in love?'

I shrug. 'Yes ... a bit. But I'll have to get rid of him eventually.' I sound harder and crueller than I ever could be, and Esther accepts my performance with a smile, tilting her head back and pouring the last drop of honey-coloured wine down her throat.

'Of course, sweetie. Just enjoy it while you can.' She strokes my cheek. 'It's a long life and we're only beautiful for a little bit of it.' She says this in cut-glass English, as if she's reading a line from a Noël Coward play.

'How depressing.' I sigh, unable to match her line with something sophisticated of my own.

'We'll be old soon, it's true,' she says. 'A quarter of a century this year.'

'I still feel such a baby.'

'You're a babe, that's for sure!' She winks at me, and I grab her hand and say that no, *she's* the babe, and then we're off in a game of 'no, *you* are'.

She shrugs her bony shoulders and flexes her fingers on the floor, and I think of the way my naughty, heartless Siamese cat kneads the carpet with her claws. Wine and fatigue are making me blurry; I want to stroke Esther under her chin and see if maybe she'll purr. She rests her head in my lap and, as I play with her dark gold hair, I know she can read my mind and feel my fears: that I'm in a marriage I can never leave. That the only way forward is to fight through and make it work.

'You know I love Isaac,' I say softly.

'I know you do, darling,' she says, 'but you deserve some sex.'

She's still playing at being the sophisticate, but really we're both fourteen again, both just pretending, dressing up in heels too high to walk in. And I'm holding on to her for balance.

3

How did it come to this? I've fallen so far, so fast, away from the ideals of eternal monogamous marriage – beliefs that made me feel like a damned whore for sleeping with my first great love, then led me to marry Isaac at twenty.

At twenty-four I have both a husband and a lover, and a small string of them trailing back through the eighteen months since Isaac and I reached our agreement.

I feel like a throwback to the seventies when we tell people, usually after quite a few drinks, that we have an open marriage. Isaac and I hold hands as we say it and watch their eyes widen. They always want to know more. If they're a certain kind of person, they want to sleep with one of us straight away; if they're a different sort, they get scared and wonder if we're going to try seducing them, right there at the dinner table, with an invitation to an orgy. Sometimes I see a shrewd and wary look in a woman's eyes, as if she's assessing me for threat potential. She'd thought I was safe and partnered, out of bounds. But here I am, shifting the lines of what's possible.

Isaac and I get an adolescent kick out of shocking them.

Being married so young was shocking in itself to those raised outside the church; people who had no idea about the sinfulness of sex before marriage. My friends at university – 'your secular friends,' my parents called them – were aghast at the news of my engagement.

'That's ridiculous. You should live together first,' Elena told me, while we were walking between Sociology and Cinema Studies. She was living with her first serious boyfriend in the basement of her father's mansion in Toorak. But of course that was never an option for us, with our sober single beds in parental homes, and the strict chaperoning of our time together. There would be no repeat of the Marcus 'disaster', as my mother called it.

Twenty was too young to marry, almost everyone agreed, but even unbelievers could understand the narrative of youthful love needing to declare itself. To them we were naive romantics who couldn't be apart and needed to make the big gesture, despite the dismal divorce statistics. That was plausible.

'I guess it *is* romantic,' Elena conceded later, as we sat in the university cafeteria plucking at hot chips and dipping them in tomato sauce. 'Plus, you can always get divorced if it doesn't work out. You'll still be young enough to start again. Just don't have a baby!'

'There will be *no* babies. And there won't be a divorce.'

'Ha.' She shook her head, her baroque earrings – clusters of faux pearls and rubies – wobbling and shimmering like jelly jubes in the light. 'That's what my parents always think when they get married to someone new.'

'Sorry,' I said, remembering that Elena had seen too many marriages – and had too many stepparents and stepsiblings –

to have any kind of faith in eternal love. 'It's different for me. Divorce isn't really an option.'

'Even with all your God-stuff, divorce is always an option,' she said darkly, tearing apart a tiny paper envelope of salt and sprinkling it on the new layer of chips we'd unearthed. Then she brightened. 'Anyway, if you're set on it, just think of the Austudy you'll get as a married couple. Bonus!'

In 1992, a penniless student could reap more benefits by being married than by being a dependent minor. It was the late days of a federal Labor government, when tertiary education, though no longer free, was still something you undertook with little regard for the cost, and with the expectation you'd be supported to do it. A marriage certificate meant far more money in the bank each fortnight.

'We're not getting married for Austudy,' I said wearily. At her look of scepticism, I realised I could never properly explain to her that Isaac and I were marrying for love, so that we could be together, live together, on our own and clean in the Lord's sight.

~♡

'We're going to be together forever,' Isaac said matter-of-factly, three weeks after we'd first crashed into each other at an inner-city Melbourne prayer meeting. We'd seen the light in each other's eyes, started talking that night and hadn't stopped since. Now we were cuddling, fully clothed, under the covers of his narrow bed, our ears open in case the front door should signal his parents' return.

He kissed me deeply with his beautiful downturned mouth, red like a girl's, and I watched him as he gave himself up to it. Wrapping my legs around him, I felt him hard against my thigh. I put my hands on the hot, smooth skin of his back where his jeans didn't meet his shirt, and dug my fingernails in.

'It's so hard to wait,' he said, finally.

'I know, believe me.' I dug in a little deeper. 'But we agreed we would.'

He bit my earlobe gently. 'It's just ... we're going to get married. As soon as we can. Does it really matter?'

'You were the one who said it was black and white: "One flesh in the eyes of God – there's just no grey area about it in the Bible."' I mimicked the authoritative voice he used whenever he argued scripture.

'And I'm thinking that in God's eyes, we'll be married if we do it, and then we'll be married properly later. So what's the problem?'

'You know that I've been here before, with this exact same argument,' I said. 'You laughed at my dodgy logic when I told you about it.'

'I've changed my mind – it's actually very sound logic,' said Isaac. 'I just hate it that you were there already, with someone else. The wrong person.'

I thought of Marcus, a fleeting glimpse of his big grin, his beautiful brown body, always on the move – and his wandering attention span. How could I have believed that we would make a marriage from the attraction of such opposites? Now I saw his otherness, his foreignness. He would never have fit into my Melbourne life the way Isaac already did. Isaac had read the same books as me and wanted the same things: a life full of ideas and writing and talking. And even though we all lived in Melbourne now, Isaac's parents and mine knew one another from high school in Perth. It seemed as if destiny – no, God's plan! – had brought us to the same city.

I'd moved to Melbourne six months earlier, when Dad had taken another 'call' and transferred from Perth. I'd decided to join him, along with my mother and brother, and we set up home in the bleak outer-eastern suburbs where the sky always seemed low and grey. It was my first year at uni. I missed the beach and the bright blue skies of Perth – and Esther and Claudia, of course – but felt I had no choice. I still needed my parents, and I needed a new life away from Marcus and the mess we'd made. I could start fresh; I could be good again. Marcus left too, for Sydney.

In Melbourne I started reading my Bible every morning and praying myself to sleep. I imagined my thoughts floating upwards like incense in an act of worship. I struggled with the right voice to adopt when speaking to Jesus, wondering how formal I should be. I knew he loved us intimately – he knew by name every sparrow that fell from its nest, so how much more did he care for us humans, who were only 'a little lower than the Angels'?

All my life I'd been told that Jesus read my thoughts and watched my every action; that he cried when I sinned, and smiled when I spoke to him. I thought of him as a mix between an all-knowing father and an all-seeing friend. Surely he could accept colloquialisms – Jesus was modern, in his day, and he would be in ours – but I suspected he enjoyed the biblical prose style. After all, the Bible was his inspired word. So I mixed up my prayers with scriptural phrases that flowed from my tongue in a river of clichés. I'd drunk them in with my mother's milk, and listened to my father's prayers and sermons every day of my nineteen years. They were part of the way I formed my thoughts; I truly loved the language of the King James edition.

'O Father who art in Heaven, hallowed be thy name ...' I'd begin by naming things I was grateful for: health and family, enough food and a roof over my head; avoiding that car accident and passing that multiple choice test. I moved on to asking for forgiveness: for my selfishness and vanity; for losing my temper with my annoying brother; for breaking the Sabbath and watching TV before sunset; and thinking lustful thoughts as I read *Cleo*'s feature quiz on 'How to Please a Man with Your Mouth'. (I was trying not to touch myself. Sometimes I managed a month or two, but I was weak.)

Next were the prayers for others: poor and homeless people; missionaries working in the Pacific; and Adventists in Russia and China, where they might lose their lives for their faith. I still worried, often, if I'd be strong enough to stay true to the faith with a gun against my head. In the imminent End Times, there would be a persecution of the faithful, and I hoped I wouldn't weaken with fear.

Finally, as I'd been taught was protocol, the selfish requests came last: 'Please help me to study harder, be stronger, to know how to serve you better. Please guide me and show me what to do.' For I had no idea what to do with my life; I was so afraid of choosing the wrong path. If only God would give me a sign.

Along with my textbooks on cinema and journalism, English literature and postmodern poetry, I'd been reading the purple prose of the prophetess Ellen G White. Her nineteenth-century teachings and 'visions' informed the birth of Seventh-day Adventism, shaping beliefs such as an emphasis on health and clean living. My parents had two bookshelves devoted to her burgundy, fake-leather-bound volumes. With titles such as *Steps to Christ*, *The Great Controversy* and *Counsels on Diet and Foods*, they covered everything from nutrition to marriage to child-rearing, to prophecies about the end of the world and what the Book of Revelation really meant.

My friends and I had sniggered at Ellen G White's work when it was assigned to us in high school Bible Studies. (We called her 'egg-white' and felt thrilled at the blasphemy.) We were especially amused by the fact that young Ellen's 'visions' had begun in childhood after she'd been hit on the head with a rock. 'She was so disfigured that her own father didn't recognise her,' Esther would recite with glee.

But now I was reading Ellen G White with my heart open. I took in what she said about 'controlling the passions and affections', and about the privileges that were confined to marriage, and the degradations of lust. I steeled myself for lifelong celibacy if I couldn't find a husband.

At first I was friendless in Melbourne, so I gratefully attached myself to a group of Adventist university students who'd embraced a more Pentecostal version of the Adventism that merged its traditional beliefs with American exuberance and emotionalism. We did everything together: wholesome activities like bowling and camping, singing in worship bands and helping out in retirement homes.

Under their influence, I gathered the necessary conviction – and squashed my embarrassment at standing up in front of an audience – to undergo a proper baptism by full immersion in a pool of lukewarm water. Wearing a navy-blue choir gown edged in pure white, I died to sin. My father lowered me into the water and I arose, wet and new, in front of a singing congregation. My mother received me on the sidelines with a fluffy towel and a hairdryer. Soon I would be shaking the hands of all the well-wishers who welcomed me into my new life, recommitted to Jesus.

~♡

I'd been trying so very hard to be good and pure. And here I was in bed with this boy.

'It's different now,' Isaac said, slipping his hands under my corduroy miniskirt to my thick black tights. 'You're with the right person.'

'I *do* want to.' I turned over so that my back was against him and pulled his arm across me, leaning into the warmth of him. I felt safer and less alone than I'd ever been before. He kissed my neck and I shivered at the deliciousness.

I loved Isaac, everything about him. I loved his bookishness, his brilliance and his severe morality tempered with surges of rebellion that were so like my own. He'd been baptised at twelve but as a teenager had struggled, like me, with the rules. He was my match, the one with whom I could be 'equally yoked' – as scripture advised.

But we were still so young. Even for Adventists, twenty was too young to marry. It was expected that we'd at least get our undergraduate degrees first.

'Even if we announced our engagement tomorrow, we can't get married for at least a year,' he said, 'and I can't wait that long. Can you?' He slipped his hand under my jumper and into my bra, finding my nipple with his thumb.

'Let's get a marriage certificate, then,' I said, breathless.

He cupped my breast. 'What, secretly?'

'I guess.' The plan had just popped into my head that second, but it lit the way for us to do what we wanted to do. 'We'll know we're married and then we can have a wedding later.'

'Genius!' He shifted his hands up my skirt again and into my tights. 'I love the way you think.' His fingers burrowed in to find the warm, slippery place that I wanted him to find. 'Seeing as we have that plan in place, why don't we celebrate?' he murmured in my ear.

I sighed, wriggling to make it easier for him to undress me. 'I'm so weak and easily swayed.'

'You're *corruptible*.' He rolled the word around with pleasure, like Rumpole of the Bailey.

'Don't say that,' I pleaded. 'I wanted to be good this time.' My voice was muffled as I pulled my jumper over my head.

'You *are* good,' he said, gazing down at me now, naked beneath him.

I wanted to believe him, even though I knew we were stealing our cake before dinner.

⁓

The letter from the marriage celebrant, confirming our intention to marry in three weeks' time, turned up in the letterbox at my house. Reading the back of the envelope, my clever mother guessed it all. She sat in the living room with the letter on her lap, waiting for me to get home from uni.

'Why the secrecy, the skulking around?' she asked, after I'd admitted our plans.

Aiden watched from the dining room, a pained look on his face. I was going to cause trouble for the whole family again with my love life, he could tell. Why couldn't I follow the rules in public and break them in private, the way he did? He'd always kept a part of himself secret and safe, even from Mum's mind-reading. Why couldn't I? Even my sneakiness was inept and half-hearted.

'You *can* have a proper wedding, you know,' Mum said. 'In fact, you must.'

'But everyone will think we're too young and that it's too soon,' I whined. 'It's all so complicated.' I dreaded the thought of a wedding, of making it public. All that fuss and gossip. I'd grown quite attached to our secret plan: it was romantic.

'You're as old now as your father and I were when we got married,' she said with a smile. 'Just do it! Before you get into any more trouble.'

'So you want to get rid of me?' I was amazed at how easy she was making this. Now I realised that the idea of leaving home actually disturbed me – I wasn't sure I was ready.

'If you're prepared to go to all the trouble of sneaking off to a marriage celebrant, you're ready to look after yourselves. I like Isaac and he's from a good family. I think he's a great fit for you; you can grow up together.'

'What does Dad think? You haven't told him, have you?'

The idea of telling my father seemed so humiliating. He wouldn't be pleased. I was going to be such a disappointment, again.

'Not yet, but he'll come around,' said Mum. 'Besides, as Paul the Apostle says, "It's better to marry than to burn" – and you and Isaac are clearly burning for each other!' She was laughing at me now, and I wondered, as I often did, about her ability to switch between the roles of my understanding friend and my harshest judge.

She wanted me respectably taken care of, I could see that. She wanted me safe from myself.

~⊙

So we had our big white wedding. We did it reluctantly – not the marriage, but the ceremony – for our parents and for the people at church. We had all the trimmings: the three-tiered fruitcake entombed in waxen royal icing; the white satin dress edged in feathers that brought out an allergic rash on my chest; the hired vintage cars and the historic church with stained-glass windows – the church where Ellen G White herself had preached in 1892.

There were five bridesmaids, including Esther and Claudia, and five groomsmen, including my brother. There were high heels, morning suits, red roses and multi-coloured paper confetti that stuck to our skin and left pink and blue trails when the raindrops fell that cold July day.

It was perfect and horrible. I shocked myself with tears of happiness as I walked down the aisle knowing it would be forever; that Isaac would be the only man I'd ever love like this, and the last one I'd sleep with. We pledged to have and to hold, forsaking all others, till death do us part; we ditched the line about obedience because we'd both been reading Germaine Greer that year. Then we scratched our names on the watermarked parchment certificate with Isaac's old calligraphy pen.

Afterwards there was the sober lunchtime banquet with no alcohol, no meat and no dancing. A string quartet sawed away at Vivaldi and Mozart, and Isaac was busy with his hundreds of relatives, many of whom I'd only met at the engagement party. I clung to Esther and Claudia, who sat beside me at the bridal table picking at their food and longing for champagne. They knew few of the guests and made me laugh with their whispered observations of my prayer group friends. 'They're so daggy – do they know what you're really like?' asked Esther between mouthfuls of dry mushroom and nut loaf, and sips of fizzy grape juice served in white wine goblets.

'I'm *good* now, remember?' I said, and she looked at me with a wry, disbelieving smile. I stuck out my tongue at her.

The best man's speech was interminable and unfunny, with jokes about 'lucky Isaac later on tonight'. As the guests turned to stare at me, I felt like a child bride on display for ritual sacrifice. I imagined them picturing me being deflowered later on; the idea of my sex life being so sanctioned nauseated me. Esther took my hand under the table, squeezing it. 'It'll all be over soon,' she whispered.

When Isaac and I finally fled the reception in the back seat of an old white Jaguar, his brother driving us to the hotel in Exhibition Street, I waved to the girls. I almost wished they could come with us; I saw them so rarely since I'd moved to Melbourne that it seemed a tragedy they'd be in town that night without me.

But then Isaac grabbed my hand and kissed it. 'Hello, wife,' he said, and I looked up at him as if I hadn't seen him properly all day.

'Hello, husband.'

We grinned. Not so much with happiness, as with relief. It was done.

~⌒

The relief of being married. We knew we were still children, and we delighted in that. Like kids whose parents haven't come home yet, we spent our money on toys and sometimes went hungry, but there was always more at the end of the fortnight and we had each other, so that was enough.

We promised ourselves that we would never, ever create new children – for that would make us parents, a horrible idea. 'The world is too full of babies,' I'd said to our minister during a premarital counselling session. At uni I'd been reading about environmentalism and Zero Population Growth: there was no way I would add to the problems of a crowded world that could never feed everyone properly.

'I just want to be a kid myself, forever,' Isaac put in, obviously hoping this was controversial.

The minister looked at us dubiously across the table, where his wife had served decaf coffee and a plate of Anzac biscuits. 'You can change your minds later,' he said. 'But as long as you both change your minds together, okay?'

Nobody else understood, but the two of us agreed it would be hideous to take up the roles of mother and father when we would always be so busily engaged in play with each other. We would be that legendary couple who married young and never parted. We were the clever children, we thought, the ones with the key to the Garden of Eden. Because our love was real, we could bypass the angel with the flaming sword, sneak in and out, and take the fruit whenever we wanted or needed it. Our own special pact, built on pure belief, would protect us from the creeping bourgeois boredom we saw in other couples. We imagined that they must yearn for what we had, longing for what they'd glimpsed in their own youthful romances. But ours would last. We had no doubt.

We envisaged our distant future and saw ourselves: a tall, thin old man, courtly and gentle, and a bird-boned lady, her hair in a bun and eyes still bright, walking hand in hand, and talking, always talking. Our passionate debates would drown out the creakings of decrepitude as we faded into the happy death of united souls. And when Jesus returned to earth to claim his own, we'd be drawn up from our graves into Heaven, made young again and reunited, and 'the lamb would lay down with the lion' – though we never spoke of it quite like that, because even then we knew it sounded ridiculous.

While we were still children together in those first couple of years after the wedding, we ran and rushed and played until we were exhausted. We lived like we'd been let out of jail, which in a way we had been. Free from our parents' houses, we listened to the music that was supposed to have devil possession written into it – especially if you played it backwards. We laughed at how innocent the Beatles, Stones and Eagles were, though they still formed the repertoire of many a minister's warnings on the evils of rock *and* roll.

We read the kinds of books we'd had to read in secret before – fantasy and horror and philosophy; books with sex and vampires, violence and nihilism. 'Decadent' was a word we finally came to understand as we swooned at the discovery of Wilde, Baudelaire and all those others who'd lived without limits and loved Art above morality and utility.

We went to the cinema whenever we could, and joked about Ellen G White's admonishment that your guardian angel never sets foot in such places. Our eyes were greedy and uncritical. We borrowed huge unsteady piles of videos, trying to catch up on the classics we'd read about. The images, beautiful and shocking, drew us into the dark and we never wanted to leave. I wondered if it might be possible to craft a life around my newfound love for cinema.

'Let us eat flesh,' Isaac proclaimed one day at the supermarket.

And so we ate all the unclean meats: great feasts of mussels and prawns and oysters, those dirty creatures prohibited by Leviticus for their lack of fins and scales. We cooked sausages and bacon from the filthy pig, an animal that sports the necessary cloven hoof but doesn't chew its cud. We drank it down with the demon liquor till we were sick, holding each other's hair back as we retched into the toilet bowl with the rituals of first drunkenness.

Then we lay in bed reading for days, testing the limits of slothfulness. Brought up in the proud Protestant work ethic – where reading a book was a waste of time unless it was useful or spiritually uplifting – we knew that reading for pleasure was an act of defiance. So we set up our bed like a becalmed pleasure cruiser, stacking it with the tools of idleness: magazines, videos and books. When we grew tired of them, we kicked them onto the floor and dove under the covers to find each other's bodies again, warm and alive and willing. And the constant surprise that this, *this* was allowed now.

Putting our heads together on the pillows, we let our long hair tangle into one dark mass and cried for the things we'd missed out on: the lovers, the share houses, the dope-smoking freedom we thought was supposed to come with youth and university. And we sighed with relief that it wasn't too late. There would be no other lovers for us, but in everything else we'd be greedy and take what we wanted, taste those things that had been denied us. And we'd do it together.

'The path of excess leads to the tower of wisdom,' said Isaac, quoting Blake as he sloshed more red wine into his glass and pondered his chess move across the table from me.

'Moderation is a fatal thing,' I countered with Wilde. 'Nothing succeeds like excess.' I skipped my wooden knight into enemy territory, knowing I was going to be beaten very quickly.

We desperately wanted to believe these heresies, but whenever we indulged we were still amazed that no punishments fell upon our heads. We looked in the mirror for signs of our sin and found none. Our cheeks were as round and smooth as apples and our eyes were clear. We held up our wedding rings to the light and knew they held magic that would bind us together forever.

⁓

But the Bible, the Bible, it was still our book. And for a time after the wedding, perhaps two years, we still took ourselves, hungover, off to church each Saturday morning. We prayed with half-closed hearts, thighs pressed close on the cold pews, as we studied the scriptures. Isaac already knew them well: he loved their poetry and understood their complex logic as if they were his second language. He'd read aloud at church, dressed up in his suit and tie, and his booming voice would put in the pauses where they needed to be. Then he'd offer his own commentary, making salient points on how the New Testament related to the Old and what this meant for us in the twentieth century.

At home, Isaac and I searched for the gaps in the rules, spaces that might allow us to keep the faith of our fathers while living the way that we wanted. But there were no escape hatches, no air-pockets in that all-absorbing religion that had answers to every question and biblical references to back them up.

We enjoyed listening to our progressive friends, the ones who talked about Jesus being cool. We considered their arguments about how it didn't really matter if you went to church on Saturday or Sunday, and how you could read the Bible as a metaphor and live its principles without believing that every word had been inspired by divine providence. You could believe in evolution and still believe in Jesus, they said. But we knew better; you either swallowed it whole or not at all – seven days of Creation, the Cross, Original Sin and the imminent Second Coming of Christ.

And we were choking on the huge and literal bulk of it.

'It's just so ugly,' I said to Isaac as we drove home from church. I kicked off my black stiletto high heels. 'Bourgeois and suburban and ... *beige*.'

'But does that mean it isn't true?' asked Isaac, pulling onto the freeway.

'I just hate going there every week,' I said sulkily. 'The dreary hymns. The sermons I've heard a million times before and those little stories with the morals at the end of them.'

'They're called "homilies", darling.'

'Yes, I hate the homilies. And I hate the way the men speak and the women just listen.' I glanced at him. 'I don't want to go there anymore.'

'You want us to try another congregation?' he asked, though I knew he loved his old church; the elderly ladies there had known him since he was a baby. 'We could look for something younger, more progressive –'

'The modern ones are even worse! They make me sick with their happy-clappy prayer meetings. Wearing jeans and sneakers to church and bragging about their "close personal relationships" with Jesus and how he helped them avoid a parking fine.' I thought for a moment of my prayer group friends, the ones who'd been so kind to me when I first moved to Melbourne and knew nobody. I felt cruel and disloyal. But those sweet people were so far from understanding me now.

'I know what you mean.' Isaac twisted the radio dial until it stopped at Triple J, where The Cranberries were singing 'Linger'. He turned it up loud and sang along, then stopped to say, 'At least the old churches have theatre and tradition, and aren't playing electric guitars from the pulpit.'

'But I hate the old ways *and* the new ways,' I said, turning the volume down so we could keep talking. 'I dread every Friday night when the Sabbath comes in, and I'm tired of going out to prayer group on Wednesdays. It feels so fake.'

'It is a bit ugly,' he conceded. 'Didn't Einstein say that if something is true, it should be beautiful as well?' Isaac sounded as though he suspected it was bullshit, inviting me to collaborate.

I gave him half a smile. I thought of Jesus and the way he'd died just for me, but also for every other person in the world. I'd used to think that *was* kind of beautiful, especially the way Dad told it. Beautiful and true. But going to uni and mixing with 'non-Adventists' for the first time, I'd been stunned to realise that they believed their own stories with just as much passion and conviction.

It hurt me to think the Bible mightn't be true. It hurt even more to think Adventism, which had shaped every move my family had ever made, might be just another interpretation, mixed in with End Times hysteria that had sprouted from tacky American nineteenth-century revivalism.

I couldn't face these thoughts yet, so I turned up the music again and let us drift away into the afternoon, where we weren't exactly keeping the Sabbath, but we weren't forgetting it either.

The fact was, we were no longer living our beliefs; Adventism was just too plain and strict a meal to swallow. Whether or not we believed God's Truth – and I think I still did then, in my secret heart – we didn't like it and we wouldn't have it. We'd spit it out and leave the table like disgusted children, to starve or find something else on our own.

So we left. With as little fuss as possible. We stopped going to church, and we stopped praying, and we put away the leather-bound Bibles so lovingly inscribed by our parents. We began to disengage from that vast network of people who'd known us since we were eggs – a network that extended across the country and around the world. We told white lies, pretending to be sick, to be busy, except when convention and parental expectation absolutely demanded that we attend: weddings, funerals, graduations and the dedications of newborn babies.

At such events, Isaac and I would arrive late and leave early, struggling to maintain our brittle performance as a good Adventist couple: temperate, modest and hard-working. Our smiles felt like hard work. We'd speed away as fast as we could, shedding masks and costumes in our wake. We couldn't have done it on our own, but together we'd joined hands and jumped off the cliff, borrowing each other's courage.

We were young and strong and curious and we had each other. Our essential innocence would protect us, we thought.

And then, one day, a couple of years down that path, when the thrill of each other was muted by familiarity, we lay like two tired children in the late afternoon sunshine of our bedroom. In the litter of cushions and weekend papers, our two soft-bodied cats dozed with abandon. The sound of winter's sleeping buzzed warmly from the carpet as the central heating cranked on. I looked into Isaac's honey-coloured eyes and saw that he loved me. But he no longer desired me.

My world rippled and tore with the brutal, heart-bleeding shock of that.

4

'Again? You're not in the mood *again*?' I teased him. I had my hand on his flat pale belly, moving it down to feel his cock harden under my fingers. 'It *feels* like you're in the mood.'

'But I don't want to.' He lifted my hand up to his lips and kissed it, then turned over to keep reading his book. 'Maybe later.'

'It's been weeks now.'

'Soon, okay?'

'No, *not* okay.' I was getting angry. 'What's wrong with me?'

'Nothing.' He sighed. 'Can we not do this again?'

'You're not into me anymore,' I said, starting to cry and moving as far away from him as I could without falling off my side of the bed. I curled into myself and let the hot tears of humiliation flow free on my pillow.

'You're gorgeous and sexy and beautiful and I love you.' He spoke as if he were reciting a boring poem. 'There's nothing wrong with you.' He put his book down and pulled me over, into the crook of his arm, my wet cheek on his shirt. 'It's not your fault. I just don't feel like I can, and I don't even know why I feel like this. Can you be patient?'

'What choice do I have?'

'It's normal, you know,' he said, 'not to want sex all the time.'

I didn't agree, because for me that was not normal at all. I'd always suspected my appetites might be huge and freakish, that I was too much, too desiring. Now I knew it was true.

Yet later that night when he thought I was asleep, I felt the bed shaking. My skin turned cold and I held my breath as I realised he was taking himself in his own hands rather than having to touch me. Desire wasn't dead for him – just desire for me. Who, or what, was he thinking about in that secret head of his? And since when did we have secrets anyway? We'd sworn to pursue severe honesty with each other. Even the most hurtful truths were better than a lie, we'd said. So what was this?

Yes, I'd thought of other men since marrying Isaac, a natural erotic current flowing out of me, the way it always has, depending on the cycles of the month and the flirtations and attractions, never acted on, that rose and fell with friends and strangers. I knew I was built that way, making love to the world since I could walk. 'Such a little flirt,' my dad had said indulgently when he looked at the Super 8 footage of me, aged three, running up to the camera with shy smiles and a sudden kiss that filled the frame. 'Always too bold,' said Mum with a frown that told me to rein it in.

There was the waiter at the cafe on Glenferrie Road, the one who gave me extra biscotti with my latte, and looked at me too long with his big chocolate eyes. Yes, I'd wondered what it would be like to undress him, kiss him, climb atop him. But from the moment I'd met Isaac, he was all I really wanted, even in fantasy. I didn't mind too much if he thought of others – after all, until death do us part was a very long time, and who could legislate desire? – as long as he thought of me mostly, and wanted me too. But now he didn't.

He finished quickly, then scrunched tissues out of the box beside our bed to mop up the wetness, moving closer to me and throwing his arm across my hip before falling into a deep and easy sleep. The betrayal felt enormous and bewildering, a black sticky mess I couldn't understand or fight, and I shut my eyes tight in the dark, as if I could push it away by pure force of denial.

~

'You need suspenders and stockings,' said Elena knowingly, when I confessed the dilemma six months later. 'Real stockings do the trick every time.'

'Tried it,' I said, sounding weary. I thought of all the uncomfortable pieces of black lace in my drawer, symbols now of failure and rejection.

'Do you reckon he's gay?'

'No, he told me it's not boys he wants, and there's no sign of it.' His cock had stayed soft while we'd watched some boy-on-boy porn with our gay friends.

'If I were a boy or a lesbian, I'd want you,' Elena announced generously, peering into the little mirror she kept in her handbag and smearing on a fresh layer of brick-red Poppy King lipstick.

'Thanks, sweetie,' I said. 'That's reassuring.'

I felt so helpless.

I felt the shame of it. And then the anger. As the months wore on I raged and I screamed and I broke things. I threw our framed wedding photo against the kitchen wall and left Isaac to clean up the shards of glass; he cut his fingers and left smears of blood on the rubbish bin. Often I locked myself in the bathroom, sitting in the shower recess, my head on my knees, until the water turned cold and Isaac was banging on the door to make sure I hadn't passed out or tried to slit my wrists.

I skipped lectures and tutorials, and took to my bed for weeks on end, just lying there staring into the shadows. I wouldn't open the curtains, turn on the television or even pick up a book. My eyes were heavy with tears and my hands felt like lead. How could I possibly read? And in my mind, to stop reading was to start dying.

I thought I *was* dying. Here I was, twenty-two, and my version of the sublime was over and done with. Finished.

I was a pit of need and I hated myself. I knew that the more desperate I became – the more I asked for it – the less he wanted me, and the more he retreated into himself and to his study. There he'd be for hours with the door shut, headphones clamped to his ears, listening to the same music over and over – that winter it was Pink Floyd's *The Wall* on constant rotation, and he knew I couldn't stand it. He'd sing along as he played on his computer, simulating worlds where populations would arise and thrive and die and new ones would take their place. He could shape civilisations with the tap of his fingers and the introduction of a virus or an earthquake. Who could blame him for avoiding me? I knew I was disgusting and boring. I hated us both.

But when he emerged from the screen, he did try to make me feel better. 'Come darling, don't be sad,' he'd say as he brought me cup after cup of Earl Grey tea in the dark bedroom, where I'd turn over and let it go cold. Then, stroking my hair, he'd tell me that he would never leave me: 'Not even in a million years – not even if you're horribly disfigured in a car accident and I have to wipe your bum.'

'Really?' I'd say into my pillow.

'Really. Not even if you hate me and never speak to me again, except through notes shoved under the door. I'll still be here.'

I'd have to smile.

He tried to draw me out of the dark with gifts – jewellery and silk scarves, and hand-made chocolates that I didn't eat, because I'd decided if I could be thinner then maybe he'd want me again. I was losing weight and liking the sharp jut of my hipbones, but Isaac was worried. He cooked for me, badly, and cleaned the dusty house, clumsily, because he knew the dirt disgusted me; that his slovenly ways were just another problem in our fraying marriage.

Sometimes he composed love poems and troubadour songs that he played to me on his acoustic guitar while I sat listlessly on the couch. They made me weep with frustration because courtly love is, after all, chaste and unrequited.

'I wish I could write and play like you,' I told him, 'but these poems and songs don't help me. They're bloodless and their feet don't touch the earth.'

'The feelings are real,' he said. 'I can only give you what I have.'

'Eat up, eat up,' Isaac urged me one night as I picked at the bolognese pasta he'd made, an old, comforting recipe from our childhood, with Nutmeat instead of mince. 'You've got to eat.'

'I'm too sad,' I said melodramatically. 'But I'm not too sad to drink!' I poured myself another glass of Chardonnay.

'Look, can't we just agree I'm a fucked-up fool, and this has nothing to do with you?'

I couldn't believe him. 'It's because I'm too much, isn't it? I've always been too much for everybody. Too much trouble. Too intense. Too much sex drive.'

'I love your… *muchness*,' he said, smiling, plucking out of the air the Mad Hatter's word for Alice. 'It isn't that.' He was playing with the wax from the candle he'd lit for dinner. It had pooled in a soft white lump on the green checked tablecloth and he was moulding it into a ball before it went cold. His smile had faded. 'I just feel black inside, and it comes and goes – the way it did when I was growing up.'

It sounded as though he was telling the truth, and I felt a spark of hope. I took a tiny mouthful of my pasta. Maybe I was hungry after all. 'How about counselling or some antidepressants?'

His eyes narrowed. 'You know those things smash libido dead. And talking is useless.'

I was fed up. 'So I just have to accept this, live with it?'

'For better or for worse, remember?' He took my plate and started to eat my leftovers.

'I can't live with it.'

'Stop being such a spoilt brat, Eve.'

'I hate you.'

'No, you don't,' he said, looking over at me seriously.

'I do!' I stabbed my fork into his ball of wax.

'No, you don't. You love me.' He clasped my wrist, pinning it down. And he had me there.

We'd talk about it like this long into the night, sucked through circular eddies that led us into anger on my part and guilt on his. Occasionally, when we were exhausted and drunk, he made love to me. But it was an act of will on his part and we both knew it. The sadness afterwards was even worse than before, and we'd wake up the next morning hung-over and ashamed.

After a while, though, the sun came out again, and we were still married. We fought about the dishes and gave dinner parties. He went to work, where he designed smart games for the military, and I picked up my books again, beginning to study and write my Honours thesis. We kissed hello and goodbye – wonderful kisses that could turn deep and long. That had never changed. We held hands when we went to the movies and we talked on the phone several times a day, just for the sound of each other's dear voices. We knew that our lives depended upon each other; there was no way out. We were family. We were in love. And that was enough.

~⊖

'You look hot tonight,' Isaac said as he lay on the bed watching me get dressed to go out. We were meeting some friends at a pub in Richmond for a cabaret drag show – drag queens being his latest obsession.

'What's the use of looking hot if you don't want to fuck me?' I said bitterly, staring into the mirror and lining my eyes with extra kohl. We'd been to see Pabst's silent black-and-white film *Pandora's Box* a few months earlier at the Westgarth and I'd been smitten with the doomed seductress, Lulu, played by Louise Brooks. I'd cut my hair into her shiny bob and started making up my eyes into bruise-rimmed embers that turned messy as the night wore on.

'It's not that I don't want you,' Isaac declared. 'It's that *I* want to be wanted.'

'But I *do* want you.'

'I know you do. But …'

'It's not enough that I want you?' I said, turning around and glaring at him. He was lying there fully dressed with his pointy black shoes on the doona, playing Tetris on the Game Boy I'd given him for his twenty-first birthday. I pushed his feet off the bed in disgust.

'Men want you all the time,' he said resentfully. 'I see it.'

'So you're jealous?'

'Not like that. I know you're mine. I just want to feel wanted that way too.'

'It doesn't mean much,' I said. 'Men look, and women are looked at. Women are different when they lust after men. They're slow burn.'

'Women have *all* the power, sexually,' he said darkly.

It always came down to this. No matter how much I argued and he conceded the general case of female oppression, he still felt rejected by women. They never wanted him the way he wanted them.

'Do you want to be a woman?' I said, annoyed.

'No,' he said, as if really considering it. 'But I wish I felt that power.'

'Yeah, I feel *so* powerful,' I said. 'I'm married to someone who wants everyone except me. I'm essentially celibate and I'm not even twenty-three.'

'You don't have to be celibate.' He didn't even glance at me as he put on his coat and jangled the car keys in his pocket. 'As long as you ask me first, and tell me everything.'

I looked at him and the room was filled with a loaded silence, like the moment before an explosion. He wouldn't catch my eye.

'Come on, let's go,' he said. 'We'll be late.'

~⊘

So our open marriage came to be. Because we knew that nothing could tear us apart, and because we shared everything, we knew the longings of each other's hearts. Isaac knew I needed what he couldn't give me – and I knew that what he wanted was to be desired by other women. We'd experimented with so many other things in our quest to break away from religion. Why not sex too?

We wanted to make each other happy.

The key to success lay in honesty and trust, we decided, as we pored over Nena and George O'Neill's bestselling book, *Open Marriage*, which I'd found at the local library. 'I can't believe this was written in 1972, the year I was born,' I said.

'Our parents missed out on the seventies,' said Isaac. 'Do they even know about this?'

'Don't think about them!' I said, horrified.

The rules seemed simple and clear. Complete disclosure and mutual decision-making. If one of us said 'stop', we'd stop; if one of us said 'no', then we wouldn't. The arrangement came from a place of loving someone so much that you'd let them pursue their pleasures and trust they'd return to you. Nena and George wrote about equality in marriage at a time when this was revolutionary; about growth and allowing your partner to be who they were outside of traditional gender roles. Their book became shorthand for swinging, but that wasn't really what they were on about. Of course, like most people who read the book, we really just wanted the information about sex and sharing.

Nena and George warn that the 'primary relationship' can be threatened if one spouse falls in love outside of it. While love with others can be part of the picture, the primary relationship always has to come first.

'That makes sense,' said Isaac, putting the book down on the covers between us and adjusting the pillows behind his head. 'The thing is to have limits and tell each other everything.'

'I can't even imagine loving anyone else.' I moved in to rest my head on his chest.

'But you could fancy them,' he said, stroking my hair.

'Oh yes,' I said, already picturing the first man I wanted to try, the one I'd had a crush on since meeting him at Isaac's work party. 'I could definitely fancy them.'

We had no idea what we were constructing, except that we wanted to 'live in truth'. We were making up the plot of a love story, and because it was so unfamiliar to us, we thought we were so original. We thought that we'd found not just the next best thing to monogamous love, but a superior, non-possessive version of it. The way to be free but safe: to have our cake and eat it too. Who wouldn't want that?

We started tentatively, holding hands as we jumped in. A friend, a neighbour, people we knew and trusted; people we liked and approved of as a couple. I saw Isaac's colleague for a couple of months. At forty-four he was an old man to me, sly and worldly. But he had tricks with his tongue that I'd never encountered and I was drunk on orgasms for a while. It felt good to send him back to his wife, happy and tired – and to end our affair before he could have a heart attack in my bed during his lunch hour. Isaac met a girl at work and sometimes he'd go back to her place for lunch and strip poker. I'd feel relieved that he was having fun, feeling desired, and that he had a playmate to compete with in the kind of games I had no patience for.

Once, Isaac and I had a foursome with some friends and woke up bleary-eyed and tangled in their bed, all of us trying to act natural over coffee and breakfast, and yet, the friendship thrived with a twinkle each time we met again, though the orgy was never repeated. And then, there was the holiday when Claudia came to stay, and she and Isaac found a sweet three-day connection that gave me a matchmaker's satisfaction as I watched it unfold.

Through it all, we came home and whispered the details to each other, co-conspirators. We started having sex together again, occasionally, because now there was fresh air between us. And our hearts lay safe in the truths that we shared. We were blessed, and we knew it, with a love that would never admit defeat.

5

I wake up with sweaty feet, remembering that I'm here in my home town, back in Perth where the summers don't require bed socks, and cotton sheets are all you need between your skin and the warm night air. The mid-morning sunshine streams through the gaps in the blue velvet drapes. I stretch out, smiling at the luxury of having no large, long husband crowding me over to the side of the double bed.

Esther's making a pot of tea in the kitchen when I come downstairs. She's wearing an old silky kimono that was her mother's in another life, and her bed-tumbled curls are pulled up in a big diamante hairclip. Even without makeup she's a sparkling mess of blonde beauty. Her face looks open and clean, almost plain except for the light shining from her perfect skin and the live crystals of her blue eyes.

'Hello, sunshine,' she says when she sees me, grabbing another mug from the top cupboard.

'Sunshine yourself.' I feel sallow and washed out. 'You're all glowy first thing in the morning and I hate you.'

But actually I'm envious and delighted. I love looking at

her and knowing that she's my own best friend. I also wish sometimes that I could *be* her, take some of her shine for myself and have what she has. When we were younger I didn't know what to do with this feeling and I betrayed her, borrowed things from her, like boyfriends. Because I loved her so much. We can laugh about it now, safe in the knowledge that we've mapped out our separate tastes in men, work, clothes and vices, but back then I thought my world would collapse when it seemed she might never forgive me.

'Bring these outside,' says Esther, motioning towards the tea things. She grabs her pack of cigarettes from the bench.

Esther and Claudia both smoke now, but they'll be quitting this year, they say, in honour of their complexions, which the magazines tell us will start to fade at twenty-five. For this final summer, however, they will puff and blow, fiddle with silver lighters and have their shiny manicured fingernails on show as they draw narrow cigarettes from unlined lips.

I watch their rituals like a foreigner: tolerant, amused and refusing to admonish. They do seem to be temporary smokers. They only do it outside and complain about the smell, fastidious with mouthwash and air-freshener. But for me it's the smell that tells me we're here and now, not there and then, when our parents and teachers would warn us of polluted lungs and lives lost to the poisons of tobacco.

My father ran Five-Day Quit programs throughout the eighties, projecting short propaganda films onto a big roll-down screen. Dying lungs shrivelled with every puff; grey-skinned middle-aged men looked blankly into the camera. Dad would then pick up Smoking Sam, an egg-like doll of ivory-coloured plastic, punctured with a glass tube. When the cancer-stick was put to the tube and lit, Sam's cavity would fill with black smoke, turning the pearly egg into dirty grey, just as it would our lungs. It was a shocking effect, like magic, and my father the evangelist enjoyed the theatre of it. He was so good at it too, convincing hundreds of hopeful people 'from outside the Church' to sign declarations to themselves that they would give up the evil weed and take up fresh air instead. In the process, some of them took up Jesus as well, because Jesus snuck in on Day Five of the program, smuggled in under the cover of health.

Every time I kiss a smoker now, I know he's not my father, or my brother, or anything to do with God, and I know that I'm free to taste something else. It's the smell of illicit, self-destructive freedom. But I'll never smoke.

Esther and Claudia have set up the paved patio as a vine-hung smoking room. It's here, in the fresh morning air, that Esther lays out the teapot and two thick-rimmed mugs. We sit looking at the backyard with its faded cubbyhouse that was always too small, even when we were nine. We preferred the secretive branches of the gnarly old peppermint tree, its canopy of pale green streamers, where we'd play with our Barbies surrounded by soft mountains of tiny, sexy outfits and pill-sized handbags and shoes. We'd invent sordid plots for those big-breasted, narrow-waisted blondes. Later, when we knew we were too old for it, we'd just brush their golden nylon hair and talk about our own shameful bodies and desperate hearts.

Now we sip our tea in the gathering midday heat, and the grass buzzes with the music of sun-warmed cicadas. We've slept away the morning and yet the day stretches ahead, empty and long and delicious. Claudia comes out in her girly granny-print nightie, its floral innocence at odds with her big dreamy breasts and the wide flat hips that she hates but men love. She tells us the intricacies of her night's sleep, charting her dreams, lamenting wakeful periods of toilet trips and glasses of water.

'There's more to life than being well-rested,' snaps Esther impatiently.

'That's easy for you to say – you're not working at a nightclub until five in the morning most weekends. Sleep is my only luxury. I never get enough.' Claudia wanders back into the kitchen, returning with a mug and some Vegemite on toast. She yawns. 'What's on for today?'

'Eve's going to ring Marcus,' says Esther with a smile.

'Am I?' That's the first I've heard of it.

'*Yes.*' Esther sounds imperious. 'You know you want to. And I want to see what happens.'

'It's not a good idea,' says Claudia. 'And wouldn't Isaac mind?' She's so careful of Isaac's feelings, perhaps because of their history.

'Of course he'd mind,' I say, and think for a moment that maybe I won't do it. But he seems so far away. Would it hurt him if he didn't know? He has no links or connections with Marcus' family, who hark from a different tribe in the Church. 'Nobody's going to tell him, are they?'

'I thought you told each other everything,' says Claudia, biting into her third piece of toast. 'I thought that was part of the deal.'

'We do,' I say. 'Or at least, we used to.'

'What's changed?'

'Oh, stop grilling her,' says Esther. 'She's just going to say hello. He might not even be there.'

'What if he hangs up on me?' I say as I flap through the heavy phonebook looking for his parents' number. 'I couldn't stand it.'

'Don't be stupid,' says Esther. 'You're just calling to give your condolences. He lost one of his best friends this week, so it's only polite.'

'Do it then,' says Claudia, grabbing the book and taking over the project efficiently. She's experienced in the gentle art of stalking, having worked in banks and clubs and, lately, at the tax office. She'll find Marcus for me, if that's what I want. Even if it takes skulduggery and even though it goes against her wish that I stay clear of him.

But the number sits there innocently in black and white next to the address I know by heart.

A few minutes later I'm chatting to Marcus' mum. She asks me how I am. She heard I got married, dear. Congratulations! And how are my parents going up in the Solomon Islands? And is my brother still studying to be a teacher? Then she yells out to Marcus in her strong South African accent, an accent which is absent in her son's speech except for the odd word and intonation that I once loved, and an elegant graciousness that comes through when he's trying to sell something.

'Marcus, it's Eve!' she yells again, and the chattering background voices are suddenly silent.

Then he's there on the line, sounding breathless and shaken. 'Eve?'

'It's me.' I shut my eyes at the sound of his voice.

'It's been so long. Nearly six years. I thought you were gone forever.'

'I was.'

'But where are you now? Are you in Perth? Are you with … your husband?'

'I'm at Esther's for a holiday. Isaac's coming over in a couple of weeks, for Christmas.'

Silence.

'It's too much.' Marcus' voice is strained. 'Simon's funeral, and now hearing your voice.'

'Sorry. About Simon,' I say softly. 'And for ringing you like this, out of the blue. I'll let you get back to it.'

Silence again.

I'm about to put the phone down. I'm thinking how clumsy it was to call him like this in his grief, just because I was curious. And even though I'm so used to being angry with him, I realise how little I enjoy making him suffer.

'Don't go,' he says. 'I want to see you. But we're about to have Sabbath lunch.' I hear a voice in the background. 'Mum says to come over and eat with us. Can you?'

~

Esther and Claudia help me choose an outfit in a flurry of giggles. What do you wear to see the love of your life, years down the track after he dumped you, begged you back and dumped you again? These are fine and subtle calibrations, the semiotics of dress.

'Go for sexy but not slutty,' says Esther. 'Something that tells him, "You missed out, idiot!"'

'No, what you need is something that says, "Hands off!"'
Claudia puts in reprovingly.

'This!' Esther holds out a dark denim skirt, A-line and short, but not too short. 'It's lucky your legs are brown,' she says, eyeing me as I stand there in my black lace underpants.

'It's fake tan,' I say. 'How could I get brown this early in Melbourne?'

'I think I'll sunbake this afternoon because I'm so white.' Esther extends one long leg and rotates her slender ankle. Then she rummages in my suitcase. 'How about this top? Casual, not trying too hard.' She hands me a small black t-shirt and I slip it on, happy to be directed. 'Hurry up,' she says, 'I'll drop you there now on my way to the shops.' She flings off her kimono, pulling on one of my sundresses as she winks at me, not even asking if she can borrow it.

Then I'm sitting in the car, heart thumping as I'm strapping on my sandals and she drives.

'Are you okay?' she says, smiling at me.

'Hearing his voice was strange. I'm nervous.'

'You'll be fine. Nice toenails, by the way.'

They're painted the colour of dark blood, a shade that Jay chose at the chemist when we were picking up condoms. My toenails are congealed points of knowingness on my small feet, feet that have taken me so far away from Marcus. I steel myself to be cool and superior when we meet. We shared our teen years, that's all. We'll pay our respects to that memory.

I direct Esther instinctively, following the route back to his parents' home in Victoria Park. There it is, the old red-brick and tile house with its wide verandah, a bright green lawn mown close and neat. White standard rosebushes are lined up the driveway like soldiers; I don't remember them.

Esther lets me out of the car on the street, not even turning the engine off. 'Ring me when you're finished if you need a lift home.'

'Can't you come in with me?' I plead.

'Nup. This is yours. Be strong.' She touches my arm and her fingers are warm, as always.

And so I walk up to the door and ring the bell. And wait. And wait.

Marcus opens the door and I'm back at fourteen, face open wide with love and recognition, wanting to touch his brown skin and sink my hands into the springy fuzz of his hair. His huge smile radiates out the doorway with those happy white carnivore teeth.

'Come here,' he says, and then he's hugging me tightly and kissing my cheek, and I'm all in a tangle of him and his dreadlocks and the smell of cigarettes. Since when did he have dreadlocks? Since when did he smoke? I pull away and notice that he has a goatee too.

'You look like a full-grown man,' I say, and he laughs.

'Shit happens, hey! Do you like it?' He strokes his beard and turns his vain head on the side so I can see the full effect, shakes his dreads as if he's a wet dog emerged from a swim.

'I don't know … maybe?'

'You look great. You haven't changed at all.'

For a moment I think, You know nothing, you arrogant pig, I *have* changed. But after years of despising him and ignoring the messages he sent before my wedding – 'You're making a big mistake. Wait for me!' – I've lost the energy to be really angry or hurt. All I can feel is gladness that he's still

69

alive: merry and charming and beautiful. And he's obviously still quite taken with himself too, but his self-love has always been so childlike that I can't resent it.

After all the hellos and family catch-ups, the lunch and the tearful talk of the funeral, Marcus' father says it's time for a prayer before we go our separate ways. We kneel on the floor in a circle, holding hands – Marcus on my left, his sister on my right. His two older brothers, their young wives and his mother complete the ring. My bare knees ache on the brown parquetry, the pain bringing up memories of all those prayers and all those sore knees. I would usually count off each piece of the repetitious ritual, eager to get to the end of the sermon and then home to lunch. But sometimes, sitting on the hard wooden pew and gazing upwards at the sunlight shining through dust motes, I'd think I heard God speaking to me, whispering to my heart that he forgave my sins, and that this Sabbath was a wiping of the slate. A new week and a new me lay ahead, bright and shining.

'We thank you, oh Lord, for bringing us together,' says the deep voice of the good father, the father whose son I once loved more than my faith, more than God, more than my virginity. I open one eye and look at Marcus, whose eyes are shut tight, short curly lashes pressed together. He squeezes my hand. I wonder if he still believes, and if he's about to cry, thinking of Simon. He's never been shy to cry. We used to push ourselves to tears until we were exhausted and dry-eyed, limping away from the wrecks we'd made of each other. My mother would tell me she was tired of seeing me cry, that she wanted it to be over.

'It *is* over now,' I said bitterly, after the final big break-up. 'You'll be happy about that.'

'I am,' Mum said, with steel in her voice as she watched his headlights retreat from the driveway and closed the curtains. 'The Holy Spirit told me that you need to leave this destructive relationship.'

'Right, the Holy Spirit said that?' I sneered, then blew my nose on a tissue. 'It's so convenient when the Holy Spirit wants what you want.'

'Don't be sacrilegious, darling,' she said gently, coming over to sit beside me on the couch and pulling my head onto her lap. Her softness and the familiar powdery smell of her made me sob all over again. 'You're going to be alright soon,' she said as she stroked my hair. 'Let's try to forget him.'

~♡

After the prayers, people wander off into other parts of the house and it's suddenly quiet. Marcus and I are alone, gazing at each other from opposite ends of the sticky brown leather chesterfield. He keeps smiling and shaking his head as if he's trying to wake up from a dream. 'I can't believe you're here.'

'Me neither.'

'I'm just so happy to see you.' He plucks at a button on the couch and looks away from me. 'I've wanted to explain things so many times, apologise for that last time we were supposed to catch up and I didn't show.'

'It was a lifetime ago,' I say with a shrug, and he looks hurt.

We decide that we need to see the Indian Ocean. That blue horizon must be ritually revisited, especially since we've been away in the eastern states for so long. Marcus goes to the bedroom at the back of the house, asking to borrow the keys to his mother's old red car, and I hear her sleepy voice: 'Don't you forget she's a married lady now, Marcus. You be a gentleman.' And his reply, 'Oh Ma, we're just going for a drive.'

We head down the streets of our teens, where the houses are bigger and nicer now – either there's more money to go around or the poor people got pushed out. We turn onto Albany Highway, heading towards the city. I remember it being clogged up and ugly with too many buses and trucks, and it's still busy, but nothing compared to driving in Melbourne. Over on the left is the bus stop where Marcus and I used to meet – all that travel for just a few moments together felt worth it – and the phone box where he would call me after he'd been banned from tying up the line at home.

We don't speak much yet. It's enough to be here, in the hot confined space, absorbing the fact that after so many years we're no longer estranged.

The causeway bridge is soon in front of us, its glittering entrance across the Swan River into East Perth. I look at that perfect, miniature city skyline ahead of us, its cluster of mirrored office towers and tall buildings huddling together for company. It's a simulation of a city, I think. Too clean and planned, with all the bravado but none of the grime and chaos of a real metropolis.

'Do you like living in Sydney?' I ask.

'It's big enough to get lost in,' he says, smiling over at me. 'And you know how I need that.'

We head east, skirting the city on Riverside Drive, turning on to Mounts Bay Road and the base of Kings Park. I look for a place I remember, where Jacob's Ladder, those three hundred steep steps, meets the trees and the patchy grass that grows in their shade. It's hidden from view, but Marcus smiles at me and I know he remembers too. That used to be where we picnicked in the school holidays, forgoing the spectacular open views at the top of the park where all the Japanese tourists went, preferring the private canopy and damp ground below. Always looking for a place to undress each other.

'People who hang out in dark places get bad reputations,' says Marcus, and we both crack up. Those were the immortal words our headmistress uttered when she found us – sitting innocently for once, just talking – in the unlit stairwell at school. That was Grade Nine and people were already worrying about my virtue.

In Claremont, Marcus stops for petrol and I watch him walk from the bowser to the station, pulling his wallet out of his back pocket. It brings a kick to my stomach, a trace memory of all those other times I've waited in a car for him. He got his licence the day he turned seventeen. As he drove I'd have my hand on his thigh or the back of his sweaty neck; I'd be turned towards him, consuming him with my eyes, as if I could keep him there through sheer adoration. Those gangly limbs and that narrow arse. That warm smell of his dark, hot-wax skin. Those nimble, blunt fingers, crime-clever with a life of their own, likely to take what wasn't theirs just for the thrill of it. Those fingers he put inside me whenever he could, bringing me off and watching my face as though it was a win every time.

He was so naughty and troublesome. A trial for teachers and for his distraught parents, who worried he'd end up in jail. And he almost did.

'Remember the van I stole?' he says as he clicks in his seatbelt and starts up the ignition.

'No, I forgot,' I joke. 'God, we were *fourteen*. We could have been killed. Our poor parents.'

'Yeah, it was bad when my mum started crying in front of the police. I've never felt worse.'

'I was stupid to get in with you. Esther knew better – she stayed home and prayed I'd be safe.'

'Esther,' he says fondly. 'She could be so religious. But she was cool.'

'She was smart,' I say. 'She knew you were an idiot. I was so gullible. You turned up at the end of my street in this shiny maroon van, and I jumped in and asked you as we drove off if you had a licence.'

'What did I say? Did I lie?'

'You said to me, "Is Moby Dick a fish?" in the same way you'd ask if the pope was a Catholic. I was confused. Was Moby Dick a fish? Technically no, but colloquially yes.'

'Ha. You wanted to believe me. As if a fourteen-year-old would have a licence! And I wanted to be honest,' he says, pleased at the recollection. 'That was quite smart of me.'

'Not really,' I say, thinking of the week that he evaded the police, parking the van down the street from his house at night and driving it to school in the morning, where he'd make me keep the keys in the pocket of my grey tunic in case he was questioned. For a smart girl I could be so stupid – I was told this often, by my teachers and parents – giving up logic whenever it proved unpoetic, inconvenient or banal. Do I still do that, I wonder?

'I was so gullible and innocent,' I say. 'I'd never even shoplifted a lolly or smoked a cigarette. Actually, I still haven't.'

'I loved that about you. The Minister's daughter, so quiet and good. But never as good as people thought you were.'

I grin. 'Well, they didn't think I was that good after I met you. But at least I never went to children's court.'

We can laugh about it now, as we drive towards the sea, but it was no laughing matter when he turned up subdued at school the morning after he was caught; he'd been questioned long into the night by the police. Our parents, forced to confer in an awkward lounge-room meeting, decided it would be best to keep us apart over the long Christmas holidays. And of course we thought we were Romeo and Juliet – we would die of the separation!

But in the three years after that, our frequent separations were of our own making, as we failed to connect on any practical level. Me, uptight and punctual. Marcus, languid and sociable and always two hours late. So unreliable it drove me crazy. Me, with my tidy head down at school, reading everything I could get my hands on; Marcus, out of school as fast as he could after Year Eleven and into a sales job that required only his smiles and his quick, friendly tricks.

Still, whenever we made it into the same time and place, alone together, past our squabbling over trivialities, when we finally managed to be alone, on the phone, or in the stairwell, or lying in the park – it was as smooth and easy as runny honey. There we had our words, the words, always the words, and we played with them like kids with a bunch of blocks, building them into a bridge across our differences. We'd chant the story of us until we'd spun it into a pair of feather-light wings that carried us both high above the ground.

Back on earth there were our bodies, and we watched in awe as they changed before our eyes. Alone, I knew the horror of mine, the indignity of adolescent transformations. But when Marcus saw me, he saw only beauty. And because he had no shame about his own body, I could let go of mine.

'Do you actually like the taste?' I asked, wincing as he raised his face from between my legs, the first time he went there. We were fifteen.

'I love it,' he said, wiping his mouth with the back of his hand. 'It tastes like you.' And then he buried himself again, going in for more so there was no doubting he liked it.

After we started having sex, we'd look down at our limbs and fingers entwined, cream and chocolate, and see that we were made from the same stuff, created on the same scale, with fine bones and narrow wrists and bits that fit together with anciently wrought precision. We fancied that our generous God had made us for each other, two perfect halves of a whole, clearly destined for matrimony.

But of course our wedding never came. My mother cried when she found condoms in my desk drawer – 'I was looking for a pencil,' she said unconvincingly – and my father wouldn't look at me or speak to me for a month, except to say it must never happen again while I lived under his roof. 'You can wait for marriage, like every other decent person, and pray for forgiveness,' he said severely, staring past my right shoulder. 'The tragedy is that Marcus is never going to be the man for you.'

Our love withered in the humiliating light of adult supervision. And my father was right on that last point: without the sex to smooth our way, Marcus and I began to see our incompatibility. After a while, the tears sank us and he let go of me. And I hated him for it, even as I felt some relief at being able to float alone into an alternate, easier future. But the staggering grief of it. My first grief.

Now we sigh as we finally see the blue sea. We watch the beachgoers being swept up to the car park by a stiffening breeze, towels aflutter and faces whipped by wet hair. On a grassy hill above the ocean, kite-flyers set rainbow ribbons aloft in the wind. Marcus feels the pull; I can see it in his eyes. He wants to fly those kites and meet those people, and he can't quite understand how I don't want to. Instead I will be his audience, as I've been so many times before, at first fascinated but quickly bored and resentful – when will he watch *me*?

I stay in the car, out of the wind, and watch him befriend these strangers, see them warily greet him, then warm to him. They hand their kites over, and I glimpse his laughing face as he lifts the paper bird to the sunshine. He waves at me and I smile, letting him be the lovely selfish clown. These habits have no pull on me anymore, no repercussions. They don't warn of any future as a weary wife.

After a little while, he waves goodbye to the kite-flyers and they follow him with their eyes as if they're wondering what blessed, easy star he was born under.

We drive further north up the coast, away from the crowds, and park overlooking the ocean. We sit in warm, dust-mote stillness. The hot vinyl dashboard smells like nostalgia. Silence as we look at each other. I wonder if we're strangers pretending to have some connection. We know nothing of the pattern of each other's days now: the work, the friends, the beds we sleep in and the gods we worship.

Marcus tells me that he still works in sales. He lives in Sydney's west and he has two dogs. He's a DJ in a club on the weekends and writes his own music. He has lived with the same girl through two happy summers and one last difficult winter; he doesn't know if they will marry.

'Do your parents mind that you're living in sin?' I ask.

'They hate it, but they're so used to being disappointed by me. I think they're relieved she puts up with me. That I'm not just fucking around.'

'*Are* you fucking around?'

He chuckles, shaking his head. 'I'm trying to be good.'

'And does she love you?' Of course she does, I think.

'Yeah. She's good to me. But I keep searching for that thing, you know – the way you used to look at me.' He holds my gaze.

I laugh at him. 'You sad romantic bastard. Poor girl. You've lived with her for years, mundane everyday life. How can it be the same as what we had?' I gently slap his cheek, more of a caress.

He holds my hand where it rests on his jaw, and his fingers touch my wedding ring. He flinches as if it were a red-hot coal, letting go of my hand. 'What about you? Are you happy with …?' He can't even say the name.

'Isaac.'

'Is it the real thing, with *Isaac*?'

I look out at the ocean and wonder which answers will suit him, how much truth he can handle.

'I love him,' I say, feeling loyal all of a sudden to my husband and the life we've built together in Melbourne, the life I haven't thought about in the last few hours.

'I heard he's a genius.' Marcus fiddles with the car's cigarette lighter, pushing in the button so it will get hot and red. He wants a smoke; he's looking edgy.

'Well, he's got a genius IQ, if those tests mean anything. I love his mind.'

'And he's good to you?'

'He is. He looks after me.' I think of the way Isaac reads me to sleep at night, and brings me medicine when I'm sick with the constant colds and flus of Melbourne winters; the way he edits my assignments and helps me meet my deadlines. He takes care of our finances when my scholarship runs out and lets me play while he's at work. 'He's there for me,' I add, and what I mean is, *Like you weren't.*

'So it's real, then?' Marcus asks. I can tell he detests every word I've said. Is this the revenge I wanted when I hated him for abandoning me?

'Our families have Christmas together. We'll be married until one of us dies. Is that real enough for you?'

'I'm happy for you, honestly,' he says, but his jaw is pulsing, tiny ripples on the taut dark skin. I remember it now, the way it does that when he's angry or upset.

I decide he deserves more truth. 'It's not perfect,' I say, taking a deep breath. 'It's not what *you* would have wanted.'

'What do you mean?'

'Well, one person can't fulfil every desire. That's not realistic.'

I can see that Marcus is confused. He's wondering what he can ask – what rights he has, after all these years, to probe the inner workings of my marriage. He's afraid that I'll laugh in his face and tell him it's none of his business.

I decide to fling open my doors in friendship. I've been

told before that I cast my scandalous truths at the feet of almost perfect strangers, so why not him? Why not now, when I'm feeling so delighted he's back in my life? I throw the words out bravely, carelessly. I say that sometimes my husband and I sleep with other people. Loving someone, and being committed for life, means accepting what has to be done to make it work, even if that seems grotesque at first glance.

'He sleeps around?' says Marcus, interrupting me, incredulous.

'We both do. We always agree first –'

'I knew it wasn't real,' he cuts in, triumphant.

'Stop it. It is real.'

'But how did this start?' Marcus is impatient now. 'He wanted to fuck other women, did he?'

'Kind of. He stopped wanting me, and that was so bad for a while, but now –'

'He stopped *wanting* you? He stopped sleeping with you.'

'Yeah.' I swallow. 'It was horrible. I felt so rejected. But it wasn't really his fault.'

'Darling,' Marcus says, touching my cheek, his eyes full of pity – pity I don't want. 'I know you.' His face is too close to mine now, as if he's trying to make his point through sheer intensity. 'I know what sex is for you. What you're like in love. This is a nightmare.'

'It's not. You don't know me anymore.' I back into my corner, my head against the warm glass of the side window. 'I can do this, and I like it. There's no deception and, actually, if you look at it one way, it's the grandest romantic gesture to give each other freedom.'

Marcus puts his hands over his face. He's shaking his head and saying, 'No, no, no,' as if someone is trying to feed him poison.

'Stop being so melodramatic,' I snap. 'It's not a big thing. I'm happy. Be happy for me.'

He won't, though. He's too busy thinking it's a tragedy. He says that if he ever meets Isaac in the street, he'll strangle him and call him a stupid sick bastard; I'm an innocent woman, and I deserve a husband who will take me in hand and fuck me regularly. 'If you were *my* wife –'

'If I was your wife, I would have been the loneliest, angriest bride, waiting in a church for three hours for the groom to turn up. I can tell you now, we wouldn't have lasted.'

'I don't believe that,' he says, rebuked, lighting a cigarette and winding down the window.

'Tell me,' I say, a mean edge to my voice, 'are you still late for *everything?*'

He starts to smile, guiltily, the way he does when I nail his inadequacies. Is he proud of himself or mildly ashamed? He admits that he's missed almost every plane he's ever been booked on; that his friends routinely issue wake-up calls when they want him to come out with them. He even missed his own twenty-first birthday party.

'What the hell were you doing?' I ask.

'Recording. In a studio. I met these people and they took me there, and I lost track of time.'

'You see?' I say. 'I couldn't have lived with that.'

He shrugs. 'Maybe I could have changed, with the right incentive.'

'No. You tried, so many times.'

'Not hard enough.' He looks out the window and flicks his ash onto the bitumen. I worry silently that it might blow into the dry sea grass and start a bushfire. He's always been so careless.

'Never mind,' I say, wanting to smooth things over. 'We were just kids. I'm glad you admitted defeat in the end – one of us had to.'

'I don't believe that,' he says. 'Now I know how it's turned out for you – this disgusting arrangement – I still wonder …'

'Don't,' I say. Then I point out towards the ocean. 'You don't get that in the east.' The late afternoon sun is sucked into the sea until, all in one gulp, it's swallowed when the earth turns an inch.

As we're left in the dying light, Marcus grabs my hand, holds it for a moment, then lets it go.

'I need a drink,' he says. 'Get one with me?'

'Drop me at Esther's and we'll have one there.'

~⊙

We argue about which route to take. Our internal road maps are fogging over with the years, but we resist looking at the map book in the glove box – that would be admitting defeat. By the time we park in the driveway we're jostling and bickering like a couple of kids who've been cooped up in the car too long. We tumble out into the quiet dusk and suddenly we're shy.

The lights are on, meaning Esther and Claudia are home. Will they mind me bringing this relic back into their midst?

Claudia probably will. I fumble in my wallet for the key I've been given, but decide to ring the doorbell instead, to reassure them that I'm just a guest and not taking advantage.

Esther opens the door in a hibiscus-print bikini top and a pair of small denim shorts, sucking on a lemonade icy pole. Flushed and sleepy-looking, she's obviously spent the afternoon out the back sunbaking. But she doesn't miss a beat as she opens her arms wide and hugs Marcus, kissing him on both cheeks as if she's European, and telling him she'd hoped I'd bring him for a visit. Liar.

I watch these two glittering butterflies as they work each other over. Like rival magicians, they know each other's tricks; there's respect there, but also competition. It goes way back. They're both the spoilt youngest children of big families. I wonder what it must be like to grow up knowing that every path in the family garden has already been concreted into history; that the only role left for you to play is the pleasing beautiful baby; that everybody needs you to be their little patch of autumn sunshine.

But I shouldn't be sorry for these two. They've always got what they wanted from life and had me exactly where they need me to be: in love with them. When the world turns away, bored, I'm there like another kind of family, a loyal playmate. Or is that loyalty a fantasy I have about myself?

Esther leads us out the back, where Claudia's sitting with her feet up, a cigarette in her hand. Her arms are slick with roll-on Aerogard and she's dressed for work at the club where she's the hardest narrow-eyed door-bitch in Perth: black clothes and a leather choker, her pale arms bare. She won't be going for a few hours, but already I can see her toughening up for a long night of making split-second decisions about people. She'll give in to the spitefulness that sometimes sours her sweet nature.

Claudia looks up at Marcus with the tightest of smiles. She won't pretend to be his friend. Unlike Esther, she's no actress. But he's marching over, kissing her cheek, holding her hand, telling her that he saw her at the funeral and appreciated her kindness. She almost bristles, looks at him as if to say, *I wasn't there for you, dickhead*, but he moves on unperturbed. He sits down at the table and slouches in the chair, spreading his knees wide and grinning at us as if he's presiding at court.

'Look at you,' I jibe, mimicking his posture. 'Make yourself comfortable.'

He pretends to be injured. 'You've always been so mean to me, Eve. You mock me. You *taunt* me! Look at her,' he says to Esther and Claudia, imploringly. 'The way she treats me!'

I smile at him, indulgent. 'I've always treated you far better than you deserved.'

He's suddenly serious and brings my hand to his lips, that ridiculous old-fashioned gesture he adopted even back at fourteen. He stares so solemnly into my eyes as he kisses my fingers that I want to look away, embarrassed. 'Well, that *is* the truth,' he says. 'The fact I'm here is proof of your goodness.' He looks at the girls with an orator's pause. 'I'd lost all hope she'd ever speak to me again.'

Esther and Claudia observe us, bemused, not sure of what's going on here or whether they can stomach it. Marcus senses this in the air and swipes his sincerity away with a laugh. 'Of course you're still going to make me suffer, aren't you, bitch?' he says in his roughest westie strine.

I roll my eyes and take orders for drinks, tossing the Aerogard over at him. 'Suck on that.'

I walk into the kitchen to pour the wine, take some biscuits from the cupboard and lay them out with a bowl of olives and some cheese. I can hear Marcus winning Claudia over, dredging up a flattering memory from school – a story that makes Marcus look small and foolish, and Claudia look powerful and scary. She was, too, with her heavy black shoes and her big hips, and that scowl she employed to deflect the everyday cruelties of more sun-blessed children.

As I place the food and drinks on the table, I see that Claudia is charmed by the pictures Marcus creates with his hustle. Soon she's reminiscing too, and they're talking about the stolen van, and then about the teacher with the violent temper, and the one with the lethally bad breath. They talk about the water fights in the pottery kiln and the terrible sex education classes in the hall, where we were told that 'heavy petting' was a dangerous slope we'd all slide down if we weren't careful.

'Beware, beware, lest you endanger eternal life for the pleasures of the flesh,' says Esther, balancing an olive on a cracker. 'I nearly vomited when they started talking about all the steps of "foreplay", beginning with looking into each other's eyes and holding hands. *Foreplay!*'

'Hey, don't be mean, they were just trying to look after us,' says Marcus, surprisingly.

'Do you still go to church, then?' Esther asks, pouring more wine. She's very relaxed now.

'Only when I'm here with Mum and Dad. But I still think it's ... right.'

'*What?*' I'm shocked. 'How do you reconcile that with the way you live?'

'This?' he says, lifting his glass and waving his ciggie. 'It's all superficial stuff. The essence is here.' He thumps his heart with a fist.

'But if you really believe it, shouldn't you keep the Sabbath? Go to church, get married to the girl you're living with?'

He looks a bit sheepish. 'Yeah, I should.'

'It's rubbish,' Esther says. 'It's all made up.'

'I don't think so,' confesses Claudia, who's been quiet for a while. 'I can't let go completely.'

'Really?' I say, surprised. 'But you never even got baptised.'

Claudia had always been on the outside of Esther's and my religious experiences. She couldn't be bothered with Friday-night Fellowships, which we attended devoutly, and she ducked out of church when the foot-washing ceremony came up every thirteenth Sabbath. The women would part from the men, and in a separate room we'd wash one another's feet in tin basins of warm water – a remembrance of Jesus washing the disciples' feet the night before the crucifixion. Esther and I liked to wash each other's feet, but sometimes we'd be paired with old ladies who kept their pantyhose on, and it was gross to touch their wet, wrinkled, nylon-clad skin.

Esther and I were always coming in and out of conversions during our teens. It was blissful when our religious convictions coincided, but painful and awkward otherwise. She'd be drinking and sneaking into nightclubs underage, while I was off preaching to country parishes; she'd be singing in the choir and practising abstinence from masturbation, while I was madly screwing Marcus. We were still friends at those times, but always with disapproval wafting from the saint and rebellious defiance leaking from the sinner. It was a huge relief when we came back into sync.

Claudia was never involved in this cycle, but now she says, 'You don't need to be baptised to believe.' It seems her convictions were deep and silent.

'I got baptised,' says Marcus, surprising me again. 'Simon and me, together, just after you left Perth, Eve. I'm glad I got to share that with him before he died – and I'm glad that he's saved.'

'You really think you'll see him again? Heaven and all that?' Esther asks.

'I have to think that.'

We talk of Simon, and the way he died and how we're scared, and suddenly we're all in it together, like some kind of family at a wake.

Then the phone rings. It's Isaac, lonely on a Saturday night and wanting a long conversation about nothing: what kind of food they served on the flight, and what books I'm reading for the conference, and how is Esther, and how is Claudia, and how is the weather, and do I miss him?

What can I tell him? I could say I'm here drinking wine with the first love of my life, and he's so beautiful that I can hardly take my eyes off him.

Of course I don't even mention Marcus. I talk vaguely about seeing the ocean, about kites, about Esther in her bikini and us having a quiet evening out in the back garden. I ask about Melbourne. Has he watered the plants? Are the cats alright? Did he see Emma, his latest paramour, for coffee this afternoon? He did, and he thinks she's a bitch, and he doesn't want her. He wants me right now. Two weeks is far too long for us to be apart. 'Don't do this again to me, will you?'

He's sulking and self-pitying. He does it so well, plays the victim so convincingly that you start to treat him like one. 'Poor darling,' I murmur, looking out the glass doors at my friends and wanting to be free of this curly, old-fashioned phone cord. 'You need some sleep,' I say. 'It will all look better in the morning. I love you, I love you, I love you.'

But I don't say I miss him. I won't tell that lie; it's part of my own fraying code of honour.

Then I'm back outside and we're talking about what to have for dinner. Do we really need anything after the mounds of olives and cheese?

Claudia stands up to go to work, gathering her things briskly, but as she clomps off she looks back at Marcus, smiles and says it was good to see him. I follow her to her car and hug her. I tell her to be careful out there in the big bad night as I wipe a smudge of lipstick from her cheek. 'You be careful too,' she says. 'Tell Marcus to go home soon.' Then she's away, riding the clutch down the street with a plume of black smoke stinking out from the back of her old car. She hates being poor.

Inside, Marcus is on the phone now, ringing the friends he was meant to be meeting tonight. He covers the mouthpiece with his hand and tells Esther and me that we should come out with him, that we'll love his mates. We'll play pool and see where the night takes us – it'll be fun! But Esther and I aren't going anywhere; we know the shambles his impromptu nights can be, wandering aimlessly in search of fun, and we know what Marcus is like when he gets with his mates. So we link arms and giggle like little girls. Nup, we say, we're staying here. We're happy.

And I realise with a shock that I truly don't care if Marcus is with me or not. I don't mind whether he stays or leaves, chooses his friends or chooses me. I've had this afternoon and it's enough. In fact, it's almost too much already. I want him to go so I can think about him, enjoy the fact of re-admitting him onto my radar. I want him to go so that I can talk about him with Esther.

Marcus looks imploringly at us, begging us to go out with him, but we won't be moved. He says to his friends that he'll call them later, see what they're up to. But if they know what he's like, they won't be expecting anything. He puts down the phone and looks at us.

'Go on,' I say. 'Off you go. You're letting people down, as usual.'

'No,' he says, grinning. 'Tonight I've finally got my priorities straight.'

Esther sighs. 'God, Marcus, give it a rest.'

'I just meant we could all have fun together.'

'Liar,' she says, and she means it even though she's laughing – she's never trusted him.

He catches her drift and plunges in. 'When have I ever lied to you?'

'Oh.' She raises her eyebrows meaningfully. 'Want me to get specific here? Dredge up old rubbish? Then let's put aside the fact of you being a liar, and move on to something more concrete, like the fact of you being a thief!'

Marcus clutches at his heart and staggers around the room. 'Too harsh!'

'No,' says Esther, more serious now. 'Remember my silver ring?'

'You gave it to me –'

'I let you try it on and you never gave it back.'

He's hunching his shoulders now, sorrowful, as if he's ready for a beating. 'I liked it.'

'Yes, well, I liked it too,' says Esther sternly, 'and besides, look at you, you're covered in jewellery.' She's laughing now, her hands all over him, moving from the silver hoops in his ears to the two chains around his neck, one with a crucifix and the other a hideous faux-diamond pendant. Then she's pulling at his hands, spreading them out and shrieking as she counts one, two, three … six rings. 'Oh, Marcus, did you steal all these from poor girls with big fingers? But where's mine?'

She lets him wriggle away; he probably gave her ring to some girl he liked in the late eighties.

Marcus grasps Esther's hands and gazes into her eyes. 'I'm sorry,' he says. 'It will never happen again.' As he twists away, heading out the back door for a smoke, he holds up his fist in triumph without looking back. Something shimmers there: Esther's pāua shell ring, slithered off her finger. She runs after him, and they're wrestling and laughing until he hands it back to her. 'Sorry, I just had to do that.'

'Show-off,' she says. 'Being a con-artist is nothing to be proud off. So much for your baptism.'

'Written on my heart,' he says, and pours us another glass of wine.

Esther puts some quieter music on while she stacks the dishwasher. It's Everything but the Girl's 'Missing', and as that sweet melancholy voice starts singing about longing and memory, I wonder if Esther's put it on deliberately to set our mood – for what? Marcus pulls me close and starts to dance, and I pull away. Dancing isn't my thing. His family dance as though it's natural, a God-given joy. Mine do not; I was brought up under a stricter code than him. He knows that, but he won't be dissuaded.

'I love this song,' he says. 'I always think of you and what it was like here, when you first left.'

I melt into him, hoping that I'm just drunk enough to have some rhythm and not too drunk to be useless. It's strange to be this close to him and yet, of course, it's not. My face fits perfectly into the groove between his neck and shoulder.

It's all too lovely and too easy, and suddenly I know I have to have him now, in my bed, because this visitation won't be complete until I've done that. This has nothing to do with Isaac; nothing to do with Melbourne and my marriage. This is ancient unfinished business.

Esther smiles at me and reads my face in an instant. She gets a glass of water, picks up the book she's reading and heads upstairs, saying she's tired and casually telling Marcus that if he's had too much to drink, he's welcome to stay over.

And then she's gone and we're left there alone and Marcus is saying he *has* had too much to drink, but he should get home, and what do I think he should do?

'Go on, then, call a taxi,' I say. 'Pick up the car tomorrow.'

'But, I don't want to go.'

'Well, don't then.'

'But I shouldn't stay.'

'Well, don't then!'

'You know what will happen if I stay.'

I raise my eyebrows at his presumption, but smile anyway. 'Well, go then.'

'I don't want to –'

'*Stay* then, you idiot! Stay here and kiss me now.'

We're kissing and it's like some half-remembered flavour from childhood, but with a twist of tobacco and aftershave, so many chemical layers warping the taste into the present. I like it, but it's not familiar and comfortable and sweet as I thought it might be when I was watching his beautiful full lips all evening – and yes, part of me must have been planning to kiss him.

He stops and looks at me sadly, holding my face in his hands as if committing it to memory. 'This is so wrong. You're married, for whatever that's worth, and I've got a girlfriend. Once we start, we won't be able to stop and it will be a disaster. We'll ruin each other again and –'

'Oh shush.' I'm surprised at how seriously he's taking this. 'Since when have you been so bothered by right and wrong?'

But actually, he's always been bothered by what he calls 'righteousness'. Even when he's being bad, it's important to him to know just what rule he's breaking, and to rationalise it and make it seem as though he's not so bad after all. Marcus wants to be – needs to be – excused, over and over.

'Precious man,' I say, and now I'm holding his face and looking into those worried dark eyes. 'Nobody's watching. Nobody knows. There is no God.'

'You're wrong,' he says, 'there is a God. And *we'll* know – we'll be hurt.'

'I don't think so.' I'm shaking my head. 'Not me, anyway.'

'Why? Because you're such a hard-nosed, grown-up bitch now, with all your lovers?' He's holding me at arm's length, looking at me as if trying to read a foreign language written on my face.

'That's not what I meant.' I don't even bother being offended. Can't he see that because we were in love once, and because we still love each other – it's so obvious we do – and because we'd already sealed that pact, it can't really be wrong now, can it? I try to explain. 'Remember how sad it was that we could never fulfil all those promises we made?'

'Of course I do.'

'Well, that grief might be gone if we spend this night together.'

He still seems confused. 'Do you think so? Why?'

'Let's try it,' I say, and I pull him into another kiss and take his hand and lead him up the stairs. Once there, I dig my hand deep into his left pocket, surprising him, but it's just to find his lighter. I'm lighting candles as if it's a high-priestess ritual. Then I notice he's shaking and shivering, even though the night is warm. So I step back, away from him. 'Let's not then. Not if you really don't want to.'

But he holds my gaze. 'Don't stop,' he says. 'It's just that I feel so afraid. Like I don't know you anymore.'

I kiss him, so gently that our lips are barely touching.

'Shut your eyes and remember to breathe,' I say, pushing him backwards onto the bed. I blow out the candles, because even that much light might be too much for him, and I lie down beside him. We stay there, in our clothes, side by side, for a long time, just listening to the night cicadas and to our breath, our little fingers touching on the sheets between us.

And then Marcus says something, and I giggle, and we're talking about the blowjobs I gave him in the back seats of public buses, and about the times we were caught in the school locker room with our clothes half off and our faces flushed and sticky. We reminisce about the long and agonising stages by which we lost our virginity.

'Remember how you let me take you up the arse, before we did the other thing, because you wanted to stay a virgin?' he says, pulling off my skirt now.

'No! Wait, I *do* remember. I must've blocked it out.' The back of his car, steamed up in winter.

'Yeah, and when you told Esther we were doing anal, she laughed at you and said you might as well do it properly and enjoy it, because you weren't a virgin anyway.'

'I can't believe I'd forgotten that.' I'm appalled at my unreliable memory and the messy logic I used, even back then, to get what I wanted while following the letter of the law. I pull his t-shirt off and gently bite his shoulder, not leaving a mark for the woman he'll be with tomorrow night.

Soon we're naked and I pull a condom out of my suitcase, the brand Jay likes. I slide it onto him and remember the way my fingers always smelled of rubber when I came home from driving with him. I lie back, my body pale in the moonlight that's coming through the window. Marcus is holding himself so weightless above me that when he enters me it's like being fucked by a fallen angel, just hard cock and feathery hands, and none of that smothering man-mass pressing me into the mattress, the way it is with Isaac and Jay sometimes.

Now I remember I remember I remember what it was like to fly. And the words come easily, as if by rote, while we slip into that space where there's only Us. I love you, I love you, I'll love you forever. You will never be forgotten.

And as I'm coming in silent waves of old and familiar pleasure, with my legs wrapped tight around Marcus, I feel something breaking inside of me: the tie I have to Isaac, the promise I made to ask first and tell everything afterwards.

This is big. The first big secret I'll have to keep from him. It's unforgivable. I know that.

~

It's morning. I watch Marcus sleep. I remember now the way he trusts himself up to the universe, curly eyelashes resting so peacefully that I can't help but see the perfect sleeping baby he must have been once, curled into himself but completely without fear. I take a mental photo. Right now I want a cup of tea, and I remember that I'm meant to be at the conference registration this afternoon and I have so much work to do. I grab a long batik-print sarong, a fat textbook and a notepad and pen, and quietly shut the door behind me, tiptoeing downstairs.

Esther's sitting outside with a Will Self novel, *My Idea of Fun*, and her coffee. She smiles up at me, wanting to know everything. 'Is he still here?' she whispers. 'Was it good? Are you alright?'

'Yes,' I say. 'I'm alright. It was a time-machine fuck, so beautiful.'

'Good,' she says, looking up at me over her mug. 'I'm glad you got that out of your system. But you're not falling ...?'

'I don't think so.' I test my own temperature for guilt or dangerous longings. 'I'll always love him. But actually, I want him to leave soon, because I need to work before the conference. Even though my paper's finished, I need to read up so I won't sound like an idiot with these people.'

'Just wing it,' she says.

'I'm not good at that like you. There'll be all these people there talking about politics and Habermas and the public sphere. And then later there's a *symposium* on Deleuze and Guattari, and I should at least read the bit about the consuming machines of capitalist society.'

Esther rolls her eyes at me. She'll support me whatever I choose to do with my life – as if this endless study is actually choice, rather than perpetual deflection of choice – but she has to ask, 'How can you be bothered?'

I don't know what to tell her. I don't know what to tell anybody when they ask me about my thesis and the years of study that are dragging on. What is it that I want to know? What do I hope to discover? (How will I ever earn a living?) I'm still so lost in the words and ideas of others that I have none of my own yet.

'I'm learning about Australia and the stories we tell, and who we think we are and who we really are. And does it matter if we have any stories of our own?'

I'm trying to remember the proposal I wrote, between Honours and starting my PhD, on national autonomy and the changing field of Australian cinema. The world is evolving fast and I want to know if we're going to be destroyed, eaten up as a nation, a culture, a species. Apocalypse looms large for me now, as it always has, but with no Second Coming and no Resurrection. Globalisation, the buzzword of the nineties, is my starting point. But it's mixed up for me with Armageddon and the complete destruction of the conditions necessary for life. My supervisor is an environmental philosopher and I go away from my weekly meetings with him convinced of impending disaster.

'Sometimes I just want to die right now because it all seems so hard and cruel and pointless,' I say. 'And so inevitable. We're doomed.'

Esther smiles at me and everything seems easy again. She's no shallow swimmer intellectually, but she loves life too much to ever drown in the cold deep end of the pool, where I sometimes sink in despair. The things that make Esther happy are simple and plentiful. She's studying (just hard enough, and with lots of last-minute histrionics) and she's going to be a doctor; she'll see patients in an office and prescribe medications. Easy. What other purpose could you need but to help people stay healthy? And on her days off, she's going to lie in the sun and drink wine and live the hedonist Perth lifestyle that actually seems rather innocent in its philosophy: love your friends and your family; stay warm and safe and civilised in this sandy oasis, the most proudly isolated city in the world; let the rest of the country, the world, rot in Hell.

I start reading but the words all blur on the page and the book feels too heavy to hold.

'How can you concentrate?' she asks, reaching over with her big toe and tapping my book so it falls off my lap.

'I can't, if you keep interrupting me,' I say, annoyed.

'Oh, don't stress. Let's play!'

She looks mischievous, and I remember all the times she's distracted me, pulled me away from work. Back at school I nearly failed maths and chemistry because she wouldn't let me study, but then she'd sail through on the strength of a last-minute cram and I'd be so angry I'd slap her. She'd slap me back and we wouldn't speak to each other for hours, until we couldn't stand the silence any longer.

Now I glare at her. 'Sometimes I wonder if the reason I moved to the other side of the country was so I could get through uni without being sabotaged.'

'You love to be distracted,' she says. 'And you need breakfast.'

We make a pot of tea as well as a plunger of coffee, and we boil some eggs and toast some bread. Then we decide we need flowers for the table, so we grab her mother's secateurs from the shed and creep into the neighbour's front yard, dodging our way through the early-morning sprinklers and picking a bunch of roses in gaudy colours – hot pink and jealous yellow and bordello-velvet red. We stuff them into a big cut-glass jug. 'We are *ladies*,' Esther declares with her pinkie aloft.

'We *are* ladies,' I agree. 'Ladies who breakfast in style.' But we don't eat much, because our stomachs are shrunken into leanness.

We're onto our second cups of coffee when Marcus finds us, stumbling outside in search of the noise. He comes up sleepily behind my wicker chair, bending over and rubbing his bristly cheek against my smooth one, saying good morning as if we're an old married couple. Esther doesn't miss a beat, just passes the coffee plunger across the table.

Marcus sits down and picks up my library book from the pavement where it lies spine-splayed and forgotten. 'What's this, then? *Capitalism and Schizophrenia*? Shi-i-i-it.'

He opens it and begins to read silently while Esther and I look at each other, waiting for expletives when he stumbles across an unfamiliar word. But they don't come. Instead he begins to read aloud and, though I still don't understand much of Deleuze and Guattari, these abstract French theorists who perhaps make more sense in their original language, in Marcus' voice I hear the rap of anarchy and the poetry of these theories that batter my mind with confusion. Marcus loves the stuff about schizophrenia and desiring machines, and a quote from Artaud about all writing being pig shit. 'This speaks to me,' he says, looking up and pausing. And I love him for the way he plunges into life and risks seeming foolish in his quest to ride the wave of whatever's going on.

He begins expounding his own theories of 'righteousness' and 'the battle that is life'. It's all mixed up with passages from the Bible and some banal, egocentric hip-hop nonsense.

'Stop it,' I say, laughing and standing up to go. 'You're beautiful, but you're full of pig shit.'

'I am a pig in shit,' he says, pulling me down onto his lap and kissing my neck, 'because I'm just so happy today.'

~⌀

I need to get to Fremantle by two, and Marcus says he'll drop me off and still have plenty of time to get home, pack his things and make his plane. It's not my problem if he misses another flight, I tell him, but we can't be late for my conference. He nods, looking sombre and serious about getting me there.

We go upstairs to get ready. When I come back from the bathroom, freshly showered, he's lying fully dressed on the made-up bed with crappy Sunday morning television blaring. I switch it off, despite his protests. 'You can talk to me instead.'

'You're so demanding,' he says. 'You always want more.' He's teasing me with a constant refrain from our past.

'I have high standards,' I counter, pulling on my underpants beneath the towel wrapped around me, as if I'm in a changing room. The sunshine is bright and I feel shy as I turn my back to him, fastening my bra and putting on a dress. It's black with a collar and capped sleeves because I want to look like a girl with a brain today.

'You wear a lot of black now?' he asks.

'I live in Melbourne.'

'I liked you in white. I always remember you in white.'

'You need to deal with your bridal fantasies,' I say, and he laughs. Then he's watching me critically as I put on my makeup: eyeliner, mascara and a slash of my usual dark red lipstick.

'You shouldn't wear such a harsh shade,' he says. 'It makes you look hard.'

'Fuck off.'

'You never used to swear, either.'

'You've got to let me grow up, out of white Cottontails and pink lip gloss.'

He shrugs, and then looks at my bottom. 'You're skinnier now too. I like it, though.'

'Look who's talking about skinny.' I shoot him a glance – he's nothing but muscle and sinew and a stomach that's almost concave. 'You sure you're not on drugs?'

He shakes his woolly head, dreadlocks swinging from side to side. 'Not the kind that make you skinny,' he says, miming a deep draw from a spliff.

And even though I'm all clean and dressed, he pulls me down into a rough kiss and says he wants to fuck me, this time in the daylight. 'Without all the sentiment and guilt. Just because we're animals and we can.'

So we do. I worry about the clock ticking and the sheets getting lipsticked, and I want it to be finished quickly so I can be on my way. But I try to give him what he wants: animal sex. He pulls me up on my haunches and fucks me from behind. I'm dry and it hurts me a bit, but I don't protest. I want to give it to him like a gift, the one he gave me when he loved my body and showed me what it was like to enjoy it without shame.

He comes with a juddering yelp and collapses his full weight on my sweaty back. I hold him up, waiting for him to catch his breath. After a moment, he pulls out and takes off the condom, tying it in a tidy knot before aiming it at the bin in the corner. Then he rolls me over and buries his face between my legs. It must smell like rubber down there but he's got his tongue and nose in me, enthusiastically, and then he's using two fingers to bring me off. He's shamelessly efficient.

While I'm coming, I ponder the fact that he's grown even better at this. He must've done it a thousand times with girls who aren't me, an idea that once would have hurt and horrified me, but now simply intrigues me. We were here first; now there are others.

Afterwards, when I'm dressed again, I stand by the mirror threading silver into my pierced ears, and he comes up behind me and puts his hands around my waist. I lean back against him and we stare into the mirror as if we're looking to see who we are now. We smile at the image of us as a couple, an image we always loved more than the reality. We look like we belong together – and yet we don't. A shadow passes across his face.

'We've done something terrible,' he says. 'We've sinned.'

I sigh. I can't be bothered with his conscience this morning; a conscience that always springs into action the moment his urges are satisfied.

'I wanted you,' I say. 'You wanted me. Why feel bad about it now?'

'You don't feel guilty at all?'

For a moment I do. I think of Isaac at home; how appalled he'd be if he knew I was with the one person in the world he'd never allow me to see. Then I think of Jay, getting ready to join me later this week, and wonder if this would break the deal between us. Jay and I have never talked about monogamy – the idea that I could want more than both a husband and a lover just seems so greedy and grasping that it's never been contemplated.

'What do you see in me?' Marcus asks, uncharacteristically modest. 'I'm just a skinny black boy with no education.'

'No, you're the boy who wouldn't be an accountant. The holy fool. The one who stays lean with life, while the others become fat old men.'

'And you, Eve,' he says, matching my grand tone, the way he always could, 'are innocent and fallen all at once. Man's downfall.'

I push him away in mock disgust. 'You've got too much Bible in your blood,' I say, and kiss him quickly to shut him up before he starts again. 'Let's go. Hurry.' I pick up my books, my wallet and phone, and we're off into the blue-sky day.

We're driving along with the windows down and the radio blaring eighties classics as if on cue for our nostalgic trip. It's Michael Jackson's 'Thriller' and soon Marcus is freewheeling with memories about being an eleven-year-old breakdancer when he'd just moved to Perth from Johannesburg. He's telling me about the evolution of hip-hop and the aesthetics of being black. We both have our sunglasses on, so I can't see his eyes, but I watch his mouth and his lovely teeth, hardly hearing what he's saying, though I'm sure it's clever and ridiculous.

Soon we're in Fremantle and we're early, with an hour to fill. So we stop in at the Sunday markets to search for a birthday present for his mother. We wind our way through the crowds on the sea-breezed pavement, and find ourselves holding hands and licking ice-creams like children at a carnival.

'Imagine if somebody saw us,' he says, looking down at our locked fingers. Perth is a small place, and we're both breaking rules here in public.

'I don't care, do you?' I say, looking up at him. This feels so natural. It's just two hands, entwined for a single afternoon.

'Alright, I hope somebody *does* see us. Somebody who's known us since school. They'll say, "There goes Marcus and Eve, always getting into trouble. Unable to keep their hands off each other."' He pulls me in for a kiss, long and deep, right there in front of the candle shop, and it tastes like chocolate ice-cream.

A busker on a unicycle is swallowing fire, talking to the crowd in between breaths of flame. Of course he singles out Marcus to hold his props, to throw him a baton, to catch his hat. Marcus hands me his ice-cream, laughing and playing along, bewitched by the spectacle, in love with the attention.

We move on, and soon we've found a present – wind-chimes made of blue Margaret River pottery. They tinkle and jangle as we walk back to the car, people staring at us. It's almost pure joy, this stolen public hour; we've been given a holiday glimpse of what it might have been like if we'd stayed together. In our dreams.

But we have to say goodbye in a few minutes. We drive up the hill to the old limestone asylum, now the Fremantle Arts Centre, where cultural theorists will soon be hemming and hawing. Dark days ahead, they'll predict, under John Howard. But it's quiet outside the gates. No chattering. No music. Just a breeze in the Norfolk pines and the prickling, buzzing heat of sun on asphalt.

Marcus takes my hands and says, 'When you go through those gates, return to your life and don't look back, okay? If you do, I won't be able to drive off. I'll want to grab you and never let you go again.'

I've gone from wanting to cry to wanting to laugh. It's as though we're living in a midday soap opera, and I see the decades of an impossible love story stretching out ahead of us. I kiss his beautiful lips and say to him, 'I promise. I won't look back.' But he has my phone number now, and I have his. We'll never let each other go, not completely.

I open the door and step out. As I go through those gates, I hear the engine slowly departing. I won't look back; I don't even want to. I'm free of Marcus in a way I've never been before because I'm not sad anymore, that he was my first love. And I'm not sad that he won't be the last.

6

A few minutes later I'm inside a walled garden, a nametag pinned above my breast. A canvas bag filled with reading material and maps of the local attractions is thrust into my hands by a serious-looking volunteer. 'Welcome, welcome,' she says, but I don't feel it.

Clusters of strangers are talking softly under the trees and in the open-worked limestone cloisters. I drift closer to see if I can catch their words and find an opening for conversation. Everyone is discussing the state of Australian culture and the future of universities. What a lovely joke it is that these beautiful buildings used to be an asylum for the insane! Are we the lunatics, or the dwindling sane minority who see the death of what we once knew, or imagine we knew – the quiet life of the mind, the kindness of a social democracy, multiculturalism and the flourishing of the Whitlam years?

I sit in a daze inside the marquee that's been set up on the grass. I look at the people around me: women with bleached Billy Idol haircuts and ugly glasses that make them seem smart; skinny men with jaw-length hair that they flip to the side when they're making a salient point; ironic tattoos applied for maximum impact on thin wrists or lily-white underarms; and too many horrible pieces of jewellery to count. Who are these people, and am I one of them?

In the middle of the opening address by a German sociologist, my mobile phone begins to ring, and my face turns hot and red as I scramble to find it in my Tardis of a handbag. I see that it's Jay, probably wondering what's happened to me in the last two days. He must guess I haven't been thinking of him. Well, he's in a different time zone, three hours ahead – in a different universe, like Isaac. I hardly feel that they're real, my husband and my lover; that they even exist when I'm not there. And yes, I'm aware of how monstrously solipsistic this is.

I've silenced the phone, though I hate that Jay will think I hung up on him, and stare straight ahead at the stage, trying to ignore the disgusted looks directed at me. The speaker makes a joke about the future of telecommunications policy, calling me an 'early adopter'. The full invasion of mobile phone culture is still a few years away, but I am the harbinger of the Great Rudeness to come. It's true I'm the only person I know – apart from Jay – who has a mobile phone. And mine is really Isaac's – he insisted I take it with me on my travels so he can contact me whenever he wants.

Later, sticky with sweat and tired of straining to understand foreign accents, we delegates move out into the shaded courtyard where there are cups of tea and flutes of champagne. A weirdly modern string quartet murders itself in the corner. I drift as far from their noise as possible, trying to look as though I belong here, but knowing that if anyone asks me about my conference paper, I'll probably struggle to articulate its argument. I fear those questions. I hate them. I'm a pretender.

An older woman comes up to me and introduces herself. She's freshly blown in from Queensland, and her enthusiasm makes it obvious that she's a mature-age student, finding herself through Foucault. She waxes lyrical about Bentham's panopticon and asks if I've been to see the old Round House Gaol in Fremantle. 'It's such a brilliant example of the surveillance model prison, and really it tells us such a lot about the birth of the Orwellian world we now live in.'

I smile weakly. 'Yes, I grew up here. Lots of school excursions to the Round House. It's the oldest building still standing in WA.'

'Oh, is it?' she says. 'Lucky you.'

'I guess so. We had fun pretending to flog each other and putting our hands and necks in the stocks, imagining what it must have been like to be a convict. But such a big building and so much effort to survey just eight tiny cells – stunningly inefficient.'

She looks at me blankly, without even a hint of a smile, and asks if I've read *Discipline and Punish*. I half nod. I know the book she's talking about but I've only read a brief excerpt, photocopied in my Cultural Studies reader. Making excuses, I drift away because I can't stand her earnestness and the desperate way she wears her learning. I feel ugly for hating her, but my attention span is narrow and brittle with sleep deprivation and too much wine last night. I just can't be bothered. Who organises a conference to start on a hot Sunday afternoon in Perth? Idiots. I want to be at the beach.

I move inside the building, this 'magnificent example of gothic architecture'. It's cool and dark and my footsteps echo on the red jarrah floorboards. I'm taking a look at the historical etchings on the walls and the display cabinets of old medical equipment. God, psychiatry and women's healthcare had a brutal birth. I can hardly bear to read the inscriptions. Then I stop in front of an exhibition of modern blown glassware. There's a beautiful milky vase, delicate and belly-swollen, like a skinny woman with a pregnant stomach and faintly spider-veined neck. It's so sensuous I want to hold it, maybe even squeeze until it smashes in my palm, just to see the blood run and the beauty broken. It's an urge like vertigo. I want to break things.

They would have locked up women like me in years gone by, I think. I remember my grandmother and the whispered stories of her time spent in padded cells, when her mania and her suicide attempts became more than the family could handle. There's madness in my bloodline. It's in me too; I've always felt it.

'Have you seen a ghost?'

I'm startled, and I turn around to see a big man standing so close I can smell his champagne breath and spicy aftershave. He's grinning at me.

'A ghost?' I ask.

'Yeah, lots of them in here. Haven't you heard about them? Women who lost their babies. Mad nurses and teenagers with venereal disease locked up in the attic. But they're all friendly ghosts. Don't worry.' He pauses. 'Of course, they've got to be friendly. They're part of the tourist attraction.' He gestures with a lazy hand at the whole beautiful edifice of the Centre, and asks if it isn't just *too lovely*. He's obviously a local.

'You should be very proud,' I say, smiling at him. 'This must be one of the state's premier conference locations.'

'Oh, yes. The "State of Excitement" that we're all living in.'

I laugh and introduce myself, and he tells me that his name is Peter and that he was involved in organising the conference. He lives down the road and lectures part-time, and he's supposed to be researching a thesis on communications policy.

'How interesting,' I say, smiling politely.

'Not really,' he says. 'I don't think I'll ever finish it, but they won't let me lecture unless I look serious about getting the PhD.'

I like his irreverence. He wouldn't care if I've read *Discipline and Punish*. He's heavy and blond, and I can see his youth dying all over him. He seems like an overgrown surfer – beached, perhaps. Someone who's abandoned the waves in favour of books in his middle age. He's wearing glasses and I can see merry blue eyes behind them.

'Why aren't you serious?' I ask playfully. 'About your thesis?'

'Because it's not very interesting,' he says. 'And also, everything keeps changing so quickly that by the time I write up the research it will all be irrelevant.'

'Since when has irrelevance stopped anyone from writing a thesis?'

'Good point.' He laughs. 'Want a drink?'

He steers me out of the building, past the tea-shop lady and the girl behind the gift-shop counter, and out into the dappled sunshine where we drink and talk more nothingness. And suddenly it's five o'clock and time for me to meet Esther, my ride, outside the gates. I say goodbye to Peter. I'll see him tomorrow and listen to his paper, and he'll listen to mine. After that, he says, holding my hand and making me pause before I move towards the gate, we'll skive off down to the Norfolk Hotel, drink beers and talk late into the breezy, beery afternoon, and it won't be about communications policy.

~⟋

It's lunchtime after a morning of dull papers and self-important posturing. Occasionally, someone has said something that's almost caught alight, as if they've cut through the jargon into the tender flesh of the tree of knowledge, letting the sap flow and drip, flammable, staining the world with brilliance. This is why I'm studying, for that thrill. But it doesn't come often at this conference, and when it does, it dries and disappears in an instant. Soon we're back to looking at our watches and wondering what catering has in store for the next meal break.

At lunchtime, Peter and I sit out under a tree with a bunch of people he works with. He talks about his visits to Melbourne and Sydney, and the way he catches the *train* over the Nullarbor.

I look at him, dumbfounded. 'The train?'

'Yeah, I don't like to fly. The Ghan takes a few days, but it's quite romantic. You make a journey of it, do it in style.'

'Expensive?'

'Yes. But I just won't fly. Well, not if I can help it.'

It's so funny but I'm also so relieved, because I've finally found somebody smart and articulate who believes in their very marrow, as I do, that flying is dangerous. It's comforting, like finding a long-lost relative. Peter and I are talking about disasters and probability studies, and how stupid it is to compare road accidents with plane accidents. The others in the group look at us as if we're flat-earthers and move on to other topics, leaving us to indulge our fears and feed our prejudices.

Eventually Peter grabs my hand, pulls me away from the table and says, 'Let's ditch these frequent flyers and go to the Norfolk for a beer.'

He drives me down the hill in his big old car. We have the windows open so it's too noisy to talk. I put my head out, feeling the warm air blasting me, and shut my eyes like a happy dog. Soon we're in the courtyard with our drinks, and our feet up on the wooden benches, a big bowl of salty sausage and potato wedges sitting between us. We eat and talk and he asks about me being so young ('Twenty-four?') and wearing a wedding ring ('You don't look married!') – and why am I wearing such a short little skirt?

'Get lost,' I say, wriggling on the bench and pulling the edge of my skirt further down towards my knees. 'It's not that short.'

'Seriously, though, don't you think you got married too young?' he asks. 'All the things you're missing out on …'

'I'm not missing out on anything.' I'm a little drunk now, so I sketch him the basics and tell him it's an open relationship. His eyes widen and he says he doesn't believe me. It's true, I insist. My lover is coming the day after tomorrow; we'll have a week's holiday together, and then after he leaves, my husband arrives. It's all very civilised.

'Indeed,' Peter says. 'So what are you doing tomorrow?'

'No plans. I'd like to go to the beach. I haven't been yet – it's hard with no car.'

'Well, let's go together. I'll pick you up and take you to my favourite beach. Nobody goes there. You'll love it.'

'Um. Okay.' I'm thinking about whether I know this man well enough to go to a deserted beach with him, but I'm feeling reckless. The conference is over and I want to play. I want to swim in the sea and lie in the sun, and if this man wants to take me there, then he can.

~⌒~

Peter picks me up around nine the next morning. We need to beat the stiff sea breeze, which is the curse of West Australian beaches before midday. I flop into the passenger seat, exhausted and not quite awake. Esther and I stayed up late last night, listening to music, talking and trying on each other's clothes.

I look over at this beast in dark sunglasses and wonder what I've got myself into. What exactly am I doing here? But then he grins and he's transformed into an amiable bear. Perhaps nothing will happen here, except a trip to the beach. I'd like that. An innocent pleasure with a flirtatious undertone.

Then I yawn.

'You need a coffee,' he says, laughing at my dopiness.

I nod. 'A real one, not a Perth milkshake.'

'Let's drop in at my house and I'll make you one. As real and strong as you like.'

'Is your house on the way?'

'Kind of. But you should see it anyway – the view's amazing. And you need caffeine.'

So we're driving to Peter's house and I'm not sure if he's

going to make a move on me, but I shut my eyes and feel the breeze on my face and it doesn't really matter either way. I don't care about anything except sliding through space and not knowing what's coming next.

He opens the door for me and I step inside. It's beautiful, old and dark at the front, opening out at the back to a bright view down over sun-streaked stone houses. In the distance, through some trees, is the blue water. I stand there and listen to the warm, dull throb of traffic. People in hot cars are driving to work where they'll spend hours in jobs they're dying to be free of, while I'm here with an empty day and a new friend. Right now I love my life.

The stovetop espresso machine begins to bubble and hiss. Peter hands me a hot cup that I cradle, sitting on the edge of the couch. We talk about the view, about the history of Freo, about the local politics and the ugly changes being wrought by stupid developers. I admire the house. He's so proud of it, with its book-lined walls, Persian carpets, potted plants and teak furniture.

I go over to the mantelpiece and look at the photographs. There's a woman with long dark hair and a pretty, serious face.

'Who's this?' I ask.

'Angela. My girlfriend.'

'Does she live here?'

'Kind of. Mostly. She's at work now.'

'Right. Does she mind that you're going to the beach with some chick you just met?'

'I don't think I actually mentioned it.'

'Right.' I smile at him and drink my coffee in silence.

He laughs, bends down and nuzzles my neck. It feels good,

but impersonal. Like the sensuous stroke of a cat who couldn't care less. I pull away. 'What about Angela?'

He looks at me as if trying to plan his next move. 'We sort of have an open relationship.'

'Okay,' I say very slowly, eyes narrowing. I wish I could feel more solidarity with Angela, but she's just a stranger, unconnected to me. However, I do want to know what position of honesty or dishonesty Peter's coming from – I'm intrigued by his opportunism. 'You're shameless. You know that?' I push his hand away from my thigh.

He pulls me over and starts to kiss me, holding me very tight while he murmurs in my ear and asks me what I expected. Did I really think we were just going to the beach? Did I really think I was just coming over for coffee? I've got it written all over me, he says, that I'm open for sex. He wants me to suck his cock. He's been wanting me to suck his cock since the moment he laid eyes on me, so why don't I just kneel down, do it right now and stop being such a little prick-teaser?

These are the words of a date rapist, but they also remind me of an old-fashioned porno. It's all so surreal and amusing. I feel some obligation to be appalled, but I can't muster it. Have I been asking for it? Do I really have it written all over me that I'm 'open for sex'? I've been told this before, and I felt so ashamed and filthy then, but maybe it's something I can't help. Maybe it's the way I'm made.

I don't really feel like sucking his cock this early in the morning, but if that's his fantasy, I'll oblige. I push him down on the couch and kneel at his feet on the hard floorboards. He has his hands in my hair and his head lolling back against the cushion. When I undo his fly, he shoves his great fat cock in my mouth just like that. He's talking and talking about what a sexy little slut I am and how good that feels et cetera, and I have one eye shut and one eye open, looking up at him as his glasses come askew. He resembles a blond bull gone wild and stupid with pleasure. I think how funny it is and wonder how quickly I can bring him off.

But then he's pushing me away and saying he doesn't want to come like that. Now he's the one pulling off my clothes and putting his head between my legs. So it's my turn, I guess, because after all, this is consensual. I lie back and shut my eyes and think of nothing at all but the wet, warm tongue that's lapping at me.

I imagine myself tied to an altar in the blinding sun, surrounded by nameless, faceless men with busy hands and busy mouths, bringing me to a hot and salty orgasm quite beyond my control. It's my current favourite fantasy. I can't remember the moment when I stopped my childish dreaming of the One who'd complete me with Eternal Love, and started thinking about the Many and the ways they'd ravish me impersonally, but this seems to be how I work now. Soon I'm giving Peter what he wants – the slut who's thrashing about and gripping his hair and pushing his nose hard into her cunt. It doesn't take long. It rarely does for me, but he takes the quickness of it personally, takes credit for it. 'You like that,' he says, all proud and puffed up at his own skilfulness, and I don't deflate him.

It's time for the final round. He wants to be inside me, he says. He reaches over the side of the couch and pulls up a little foil packet, so conveniently placed there, and rolls the condom on. Then he's on top of me, with his great weight. I feel like I'm going to be stifled as he thrusts away, grunting, but I look out over his shoulder, into the green backyard, and I'm peaceful. It feels like a treehouse up here, and I think of the ocean. It's so near, and soon I will be swimming.

He's finished now, and he rolls off me quickly, turning back absently to give me a kiss as though he's suddenly remembered his manners. I lie there and watch him as he goes about disposing of the condom, wrapping it in several plastic bags from the kitchen drawer and then taking it to the outside bin. 'So much for your open relationship,' I say, teasing him, and he looks embarrassed.

We drive away from the house without speaking. It doesn't suit him. I can tell he's a man of many words: a clown, a buffoon, a lecturer, a storyteller. He must be feeling guilty.

Soon we're down at the deserted beach with our towels stretched out. We strip to our bathers and strangely we seem more naked with each other than we were half an hour ago. He's got fair skin that's been tanned against its will, and I rub sunscreen all over his freckled back and beefy shoulders. Then he repays the favour, but courteously and remotely, as though he's touching a stranger's flesh and doesn't want to offend with familiarity. For the first time this morning, I feel like a whore. I leave him to sunbake with the heavy-looking textbook he's reading. I walk off into the ocean. I want to be clean.

The water is cold and green. Not many waves at this little beach. The air tastes clean and I gasp it in as I swim out as far as I dare and tread water there, looking to the shore. I lie on my back and feel the sun burning into the front of me, and the chill is gone. It's a baptism of water and salt and heat. I imagine Peter's fingerprints washed from my body, my cunt closing up like an oyster as if it had never known him, as if it had never known anybody.

I wonder if any of it matters, this fraught business of who touches us, who gives us pleasure, the bodies we choose to be naked with, fleetingly or regularly. Such fanfare and angst has been had about what I do with my own body from the time I was a tiny girl, and I've let it mean so much.

Until now, I've never had a one-night stand. The encounters within my open marriage have been serious, considered, talked about endlessly, and part of an ongoing friendship or arrangement. This, this morning fuck with a man I hardly know, is strange and new. I think of Marcus and the way it felt alright to sleep with him because it was old, unfinished business. But this? I am out in the deep on my own.

As I look at my fingers elegantly drifting in the green water, my wedding ring loose with the cold, I realise I like it, this feeling of being completely and singularly myself. My heart and body are untethered and perhaps in some small danger. But I like it. And so I let myself drift, euphorically alone in the small swell, until I need to talk and laugh again. Until I'm ready to be Peter's friend.

Later, I will make him drive me on a long journey in search of hot chips, which prove to be puzzlingly elusive on this weekday morning. I'll put my feet up on his dashboard and let the wind blow into my face. I'll look over at him and see him trying to please me, and the happiness that lights him up when he satisfies my hunger and watches me lick salt from my fingers. I'll know that he's not bad or mad or dangerous, or even some minor kind of bastard. He's just floating, like me.

7

'So you slept with him?' asks Claudia. She's setting the table for dinner; it's just the three of us tonight and she wants to eat inside for a change, with cloth napkins and the air conditioner on.

'Are you talking about Marcus or Conference Guy?' says Esther as she brings in the wineglasses.

'Both of them?' Claudia looks at me hard. 'I knew you were going to sleep with Marcus the minute you brought him home. But a complete stranger too?'

'She's a dirty little whore, that's what you're saying.' Esther winks at me.

'I'd never say that!' says Claudia defensively, putting her hand on my shoulder as if to soften the blow. 'I'm not judging you. It's just a lot, you know?'

I'm sitting on the hard carved chair while she's standing above me, and I do feel judged. But I don't feel guilty and I know I should.

I remember the night before my winter wedding, when the three of us went to an Italian restaurant in Carlton. We sat in a fireside booth, swapping seats whenever one of us got too hot near the fire, and talked of the year we'd missed out on in each other's lives. They grilled me about Isaac as if I were under a wizard's spell. Was I sure I knew what I was doing? I nodded with the supreme confidence of the newly-in-love and pitied them their sequential boyfriends, each more noncommittal than the last. I wished for them what I had for myself, and tried to look interested as they told me about their studies – degrees dropped and picked up, like raggedy knitting stitches – and their backpacking holidays to Europe. They bickered about the bill (Claudia stingy, Esther skint) and I mediated and lent money, and proffered chewing gum to freshen our garlic-bread breath in the car on the way home. And all through the night I'd glowed with the love I carried for this boy who'd see me grow old.

Now he's a million miles away and I can hardly picture his face. Suddenly, I feel so jetlagged.

'You know it's eleven in Melbourne,' I say, yawning. 'Can't stay awake much longer.'

'Come on,' says Esther briskly, 'you've got to stop thinking like that or you'll never adjust. You need dinner – we cooked Lebanese for you specially.' She piles some tabouli on my plate, then a couple of lamb cutlets and a dollop of yoghurt sauce.

'But are you okay?' Claudia asks. 'Are you feeling alright after ... all that?'

'I'm fine.' I pick up a cutlet and bite into the spicy meat. 'I just need some sleep.'

'I take it you haven't told Isaac,' she says, and I shake my head. 'Don't. Don't try to confess. At least not while you're here, and he's over there on his own.'

'No, I won't.'

'But maybe you need to talk, soon, about what's going on. What *is* going on?'

The worry in Claudia's voice makes me feel the way I do when I go to the GP for some minor procedure like a pap smear, and the doctor sees the despair in my eyes and asks how I am. Even though I thought I was fine, the question, asked with such professional concern, makes me want to cry. And then the doctor tries to offer me antidepressants that shut me down and turn off my orgasms, a numbness that is perhaps necessary for an undesired wife to stay faithful. But I throw the tablets in the bin because it feels as though my life force is draining away with every white pill that I jam down my gullet.

Am I okay? What *is* going on? I'm starting to cry now.

'Talk to us,' says Esther, her hand on my arm.

So I tell them again. They already know so much of it, of the lost days and nights when I can't get out of bed for all the sadness weighing me down. I tell them of the loneliness of being married to someone who loves me but no longer desires me.

'But I thought you'd got over that,' says Esther. 'I thought you had it sorted now, with the open marriage thing.'

'We do,' I say. 'It's better now, but I still feel sad sometimes.'

I suddenly recall the pity in Marcus' face when I told him; the way he saw the tragedy of what I'd lost, because he knew what I'd been like back in the beginning.

And then I talk of whisky nights when Isaac drinks and drinks until he falls asleep on the couch, just to avoid lying next to me in bed, me with my raging need. Confessing this to my friends, I cry into my wine, great sobs, and Esther says, 'There, there', and Claudia says, 'Poor baby', and then they look at each other for a beat as if they've planned this next question.

'Why don't you leave him and start a new life?' says Esther. 'You're so unhappy,' says Claudia.

I stare at them through my tears and I see how far away they are from understanding my predicament. 'But it's not his fault. Partly it's me. I'm so lazy and needy. I get crazy sometimes, with the depression. I scream at him and have tantrums and he puts up with me. He loves me.'

'But you can't live like this,' says Claudia, pouring more wine into my glass and looking over at Esther to back her up.

'Live like what?' I ask. 'We live so well, mostly.' I try to paint them a picture of the domestic life we lead, still so filled with goodness. The treasures our habits have become, the way he still kisses me with his eyes shut and his lips soft. The way he sings to me and tries to share the things he loves – music, books, the friends he gathers like roadside wildflowers when he's not being a hermit.

'That's just co-dependency,' says Esther firmly.

'Co-dependency?' I ask. 'Dysfunction? Is it dysfunctional to love somebody?' I'm getting loud now. Groggy and tearful and angry. But my argument is genuine; I've thought about this a lot. 'I hate this modern psychological bullshit that tells us we shouldn't be in relationships until we're fully independent and "whole", whatever that means. We're never allowed to have neediness. It doesn't take into account the dark nights of the soul when you cry like a child and just need your partner to parent you, because your own parents abandoned you.' I take another gulp of wine. 'We're all children when we're sick, tired and sad. We're all co-dependent sometimes, and this antipathy towards co-dependency is so damaging for anyone trying to be in a committed relationship.'

Esther looks rebuked after my long speech, but she persists. 'Sweetie, I only meant that you got married so young … and nobody, *nobody* could blame you if you decided it just wasn't going to work with this particular person.' She pauses. 'There are so many years ahead.'

'But I can't just give up.'

'It's not giving up, it's life. People grow apart. It's no failure to leave a bad relationship.'

'I don't even know if it is a bad relationship,' I say. 'And I promised. Made *vows*, and I meant them, and I can't give them up.' I'm starting to cry again.

'Vows to who?' says Claudia. 'To Isaac? He hasn't kept his, entirely. Vows to God? You said you didn't believe in him. So why are you holding on to this so tightly?'

'My marriage is the only thing I believe in, the one thing I can't let go of.'

Then Claudia says what everybody says these days: 'Then why don't you get counselling?'

I giggle and tell them of the one counselling session we had. Of the stupid woman who sat and asked us both about our 'expectations' and talked about our 'desire discrepancy', made copious notes about my depression, and asked me if I was getting enough fresh air and exercise.

'Fresh air and exercise!' Esther hoots with laughter. 'Sounds like advice from Ellen G White!'

I go on, describing the way Isaac ran his wicked, clever mind around that poor woman, twisting her back into her chair where she sat with a useless look on her face and finally said, 'Maybe you'd be better with another counsellor.'

'Well, surely you could find a better one,' says Esther.

I sigh. She doesn't understand the stubborn immovability of Isaac. Getting him to see one counsellor was hard enough and he'll never do it again.

'Maybe you need to see a *sex* therapist,' Claudia suggests timidly.

'No. I'm tired of *talking* about my sex life. I'd rather have a lover.'

8

Esther and I meet Jay at the airport. I'm nervous and excited. Esther's curious to meet 'the lover' — as she says with an American drawl.

Jay comes off the plane looking shorn and sheepish after a fresh haircut that shocks me at first. He's wearing the shiniest, cleanest RM Williams boots I've ever seen. His pants are made of soft, brushed cotton that feels like suede when I hug him and grab his arse. The smell and feel of him dissolves the strangeness of him into familiarity. He hugs Esther too, for a moment too long, and kisses her, which is his way — so overly affectionate he confuses the delicate radar most people use to navigate differences between friends and strangers, family and lovers, gay men and straight men.

I remember the first time I met Jay, at a dinner party held by his then girlfriend, a spiky and outspoken marketing manager who worked with Isaac. We sat around a circular candlelit table in St Kilda. Isaac was at my left, while Jay sat to my right, wetly stroking my hand as it rested upon the tablecloth. His girlfriend and Isaac talked on blithely about their workplace, as if this extravagant hand-holding was the most natural thing in the world. Befuddled by too much red wine, I wondered if Jay meant anything by it. It seemed like the stroke of a pet-lover, or a gay man's rubbing of a woman friend's neck. Or a mother's fondling of a child's mussed-up hair. Confusing.

But I loved his touch and leant in to it like a cat. The massaging firmness of it, and the concentration of it; the pure attention so rarely given to hands beyond first dates in the cinema. I wanted more of that touch, even as I felt no lust or desire for Jay. I wondered, as most people do upon meeting him, if he really was straight.

His sentences veered off into the distance, littered with references to operas I had never heard, books I had never read, and films I had never watched. He quoted Hamlet as if he were living it. He told stories that got caught up in diversions that led to other stories that concluded in odd little culs-de-sac. His jokes were based on connections that nobody else would care to make – dates and numbers and coincidences, and weird puns on esoteric words. When he'd say something that he thought was terribly original or clever, he'd laugh out loud and reach for his pen, saying, 'I'd better write that down before I forget it.' The conceit of this was tempered by the way he'd write down other people's words with equal delight.

To me, it seemed that Jay was a well-adapted foreigner, trying to make sense of a culture that he'd entered late in life.

'What a wanker,' said Isaac on the way home in the car.

But I couldn't dismiss Jay so easily. His sincerity and gentleness, and complete lack of snobbery, did not fit with any preconceptions I'd had about what an art critic might be like.

'A wanker,' said Isaac again, turning into our driveway,

'but not a prick. He adored *you*. I thought he'd never take his hands off you.' Isaac smiled at me generously.

'I liked him, a lot.'

'Let's have him home to dinner, then.' And so we did. And now, several months later, I'm bringing Jay on holiday with me.

⁓

We're back at Esther's now, and she makes us drinks that clink with a burden of ice cubes. We suck at them ferociously to ward off the heat of the afternoon sun. Esther and Jay talk about music, and about London, and the places in Europe they've both been, and the other places in the world that must be visited before they die. I look on, not fully listening, but watching their faces and reading the texts written beneath their words. Jay is asking for acceptance, telling her to trust him. Esther is consenting, but only up to a point. She's welcoming him, but letting him know not to get too comfortable, warning him to watch himself and to watch out for me. She enjoys his admiration of her beauty, but she can live without it, and so can he.

Esther has plans tonight: a Christmas-season clan dinner with one of her ex-boyfriend's families. She loves to be the woman who got away, but she's never very far from the heart of a boy's family, even years after the breakup. She needs to be the girlfriend that mothers wish their sons had married; that brothers kick each other over letting go. I reckon it turns her on to think that new women brought into the clan will be subjected to comparison – and most likely will suffer, looking like neurotic freaks against her seemingly sunny easiness. She likes to win.

Esther bids us goodbye, and it's just me and Jay, sitting across a table from each other, holding hands. After a week of strangeness and strangers, it's nice to be touched by someone who knows the person I am now. Someone who connects me to my Melbourne life.

'I've missed you ridiculously,' Jay says with a grin. 'On Friday night, when I realised it was seventy-three hours to go, I felt quite desperate.'

Images of Marcus and Peter flash into my mind as I look at Jay and think of the way I've spent those hours.

'I'm glad you're here,' I say, and that is true.

I flick off my sandals and rest my feet on his knees under the smoked-glass dining table. I can see them pale and submerged, as if viewed from a glass-bottomed boat, with dark red toenails glowing to the surface. He reaches down, fingers icy from his drink, and grabs my ankle with pleasing firmness.

The knowledge that I've betrayed him makes me feel strong and invincible for a moment, like the hard-hearted temptresses of fairytales – always so much more vivid and strong than the bloodless princesses and heroines. Now I'm in a position of power over Jay, I suppose. I test it internally. Do I like it, the fact that he's missed me these past days, and I've been off floating in a haze of other men, other bodies? His heart was the last thing on my mind. Do I like that?

No, it's uncomfortable. Jay's my friend, my recently found treasure. There's love between us and it's real, even if I've put it aside for a few days; I see that clearly in front of me now. I'm soft and open, and although I'll never be a virtuous Melanie, a faithful Penelope, or an obedient Ruth, neither can I be a selfish Scarlett O'Hara, a scheming Cleopatra, a wicked

Delilah – any of those other bewitching bad girls I love. It's not guilt that I feel now, not exactly, but an imbalance that needs correcting. I want to surrender and enter back into the slightly subordinate role I take with Jay, because I am so much younger and less experienced. He knows so much more about the world.

This is my cushioned zone of comfort.

So I tell him a story about the conference and my failure to shine in the academic arena; I make him a little joke of myself, wrap myself up as a weak, funny girl with crippling shyness. We laugh about the mobile phone going off; about the silly man I met who refuses to catch planes; about the way my conference paper sank without comment.

But then – and this is one of the reasons why I love him – Jay gifts me with his own stories of failure from our week apart: the ex-girlfriend who refused to speak to him in the street; the magazine that's no longer picking up his freelance articles; the bingle that smashed up the side of his car. He says it all with a smile, though, as if these small setbacks mean nothing. They roll off him – and, he implies, so should mine. He has faith in my future and won't entertain the idea of me as a failure. He won't even indulge me or condescend to me with encouragement or reassurance.

I go over to him and sit on the floor, putting my head in his lap like a puppy looking for approval. He strokes my hair and begins to unwrap me like the guilty present that I am. He unhooks the silver earrings from my ears, removes the rings from my fingers, all except my wedding ring. He knows I like to take off every scrap of jewellery before I go to bed. Skin against skin, with no barriers.

But then he stops. 'Let's go into the garden,' he says, pulling me up and moving to the door. We stand there and he takes it all in. 'The light is so perfect. Would you mind if I took some photos?'

Of course I don't mind. Even though I've only known him a few months, I know this is one way he makes sense of his weird and beautiful world. His camera is never far from his body, and he uses it like a physical extension of himself, an extrasensory organ that processes his journey across earth. Flowers, highways, sunsets, double-yoked hen's eggs on toast, babies and dead animals: no subject is off limits. His most prized collection, though, is a vast chronological portfolio of nude women.

I can see the way he's looking at me, and I can see that these particular photos will require me to take off all my clothes.

It's almost dusk. The sun is fading fast and he works with quiet intensity. I hear a single bird, a lawnmower humming to its finale, then the silence and white noise of crickets. The smell of grass and eucalyptus.

Jay poses me like a doll. He's an absorbed choreographer, twisting my body to catch the light, unconcerned for my comfort. When the photos are developed and returned, back in Melbourne, I look like some pale Bill Henson waif with luminous breasts, pearly globes just beginning to fall like overripe fruit about to drop and rot on the damp ground. I am the girl in the forsaken garden – in danger from predators, but not exactly innocent. The photos show jutting ribs and a round bottom taken from angles that confuse the eye, making you wonder what they are, for several moments. They're beautiful-ugly images of my body seen through the eyes of a man who wants to collect me, archive me, bend me and look at me.

It's a revelation to me how much I enjoy this.

When the light is too dim, Jay finally puts his camera down and strips his own clothes off, and we kneel on the lawn as he takes me from behind. I think about what animals we are. I can smell the dirt beneath my nose and I feel him full inside me, and it's lovely and brutal and a little impersonal, but tender behind all that. And I know that I join a long line of girls and women, and thousands of photographs, and hundreds of post-camera-coital scenarios. Somehow it doesn't bother me. I love being part of that legion, and knowing I'm a link in a chain that will stretch into the future of his old age, when the women will dwindle, but his desire and his aesthete's eye will stay keen.

⁓◯

After showers and changes of clothes, Jay and I head to Fremantle in search of something to eat. I drive Esther's car like the familiar old beast that it is, windows down full because there's no air conditioning. We're ravenous and euphoric and we can't stop smiling at each other. We choose a pizza cafe and sit outside at a rickety table that lurches every time we rest our elbows or cross our legs. He spends a long time jamming serviettes under the table leg to get it level.

There's a breeze blowing up from the ocean, but the night is still silky on our bare skin. I take off my sandals under the table and rest my feet on the radiantly warm pavement. The pizza is hot, oily and salty with anchovies – his choice, not mine, but I'm happy to be led. Jay stuffs it into his mouth with greedy fingers, not wanting to talk until he's fed. When he's full, he grades the pizza, and talks of other pizzas that have been much better, and tells me of the best pizza in Melbourne, in a place that requires him to drive twenty kilometres. It's a journey he makes gladly, because he's a critic and a pedant and a champion of quality. I roll my eyes and laugh at him, and tell him that he seemed to enjoy this very substandard pizza. Enough to scoff down more than three-quarters of it, in fact.

'Context is everything,' he says seriously, 'and in this context, eating this pizza right here with you, with this raging hunger, it's perfect.' He pauses, prodding the last slice with a finger and pushing it away with a disdainful curl of his sulky lips. 'Objectively speaking, though, the crust is not thin enough, the anchovies are cheap and overly salted, and there's far too much green capsicum.'

I look at him and wonder what it must be like to live with such particular preferences; such a sure sense of one's own taste and discernment.

I am just beginning to know him and sometimes I don't like him.

Jay is fussy and obsessed with beauty, but he certainly doesn't look like any Casanova. At forty, he is ancient, I think, and he looks his age. But to women, the quality of his attention is sublime. He makes us feel ourselves to be singular, precious and yet, pleasurably, one of a collection so chosen. He listens with an alert stillness, eyes alive, and his mouth of messy teeth always ready to smile or laugh at the oddities and paradoxes of our amazing days. We look forward to the freshness of his responses, even if they're off-key or tasteless, sometimes involving slightly gruesome details of other women he has known. We know instinctively that we ourselves will become these details in the future, yet we hardly mind, knowing that we'll also be treated with kindness and honoured for our uniqueness.

There is the profound sense that Jay has heard whatever we've told him, processed it and prepared it for The Diary, which he keeps religiously, as he has since he was fourteen. We are characters in his own unfolding drama, and he makes us fascinating to ourselves, probing the minutiae of our experience. Each detail we offer is as precious as the next – our bra size, our first love, the shape of our fingernails or the memory of lost parents. He will listen to us speak of our work, our philosophy, our friends. But of course, what he loves most is to hear us speak of sex.

Sex amazes and thrills Jay, though not in the way that it excites other men, who want to be central players and would prefer it if their women had never known another penis. Instead he loves to hear of other lovers, other penises both larger and smaller than his own, encounters ordinary or bizarre. He lights up when he hears numbers – the numbers of our previous lovers, the numbers of our multiple orgasms, the dates of first and last and best penetrations. He's not competitive. Like an intimate Kinsey, he collects the data and enjoys it for its own sake. He knows each human being is another country, with corners and secrets enough for him, and for others besides.

But what would he think if I told him about Marcus? Is he really a man without jealousy? Would he want to know the details? And Peter – would he mind about Peter? He knows I sleep with Isaac sometimes, and that it can happen just hours before or after I see him. But surely this would be stretching the limits of his tolerance?

I feel myself spread all over the nation, with loyalties and loves and lusts from the east coast to the west, and no idea what to do with them. I'm a girl with no qualities and no boundaries, with legs wide open and beating heart exposed. I'm appalled by myself, but also intrigued. How many tiny pieces of myself can I give away before there is nothing left? How curiously exhilarating. It feels like vertigo.

To Jay I'm a deprived wife with a necessary second life, of which he is the current, perhaps temporary, centre. He doesn't judge me, and he doesn't dream of a day when I might leave Isaac. He opens himself up to the possibilities, and lets himself love me as if our relationship were as valid and momentous as any other. He's even a little bit in love with the idea of me as somebody else's bride: he treasures a wedding photo of me, all white and shiny at the altar, and lights up when he pictures me buying the groceries, worming the cats or hanging out the washing. 'I want to be part of the dreams of an everyday housewife,' he once said with glee. He wants to know everything.

'I'll never leave Isaac,' I told him firmly, on the first day we fucked, after a long, talkative lunch in Elwood. We were lying in his bed, sweaty and exhausted and quite shocked at the fact that suddenly, violently, we were not just lovers in a physical sense, but emotionally too. There wasn't any question that this was serious. No reticence or emotional modesty.

At lunch, before we'd done the deed, he'd asked me, 'So how does this work?'

I'd looked towards the grey ocean, wondering what the right answer was. What was the truth?

'To paraphrase the seminal seventies textbook on open marriage,' I said officiously, 'the primary relationship must take precedence over any secondary attachments, and if an emotional threat arises to the primary relationship, then the affair must stop.'

'That sounds idealistic. You can see why it didn't work in the seventies.'

'How do you know it didn't work?' I asked. 'We probably only hear about the disasters, the fucked-up key parties. There must be lots of happy couples now in their middle years, living with complicated and interesting stories from the past.'

'Of course,' he said, nodding. 'That makes sense. I know a few partnerships like that, each with its own understanding. But I want to know about yours.'

I looked over at the blonde mothers' group with their chubby toddlers at the table next door. They were drinking white wine with lunch, like we were, and their children had taken to sitting under the table, crumbling muffins all over the floorboards. The waitress wasn't happy but she was letting it go. The women looked wealthy, resigned, tired around the eyes. We could hear snatches of their conversation – toilet training, kinder duty and the trials of living with annoying husbands. The rings on their fingers looked heavy and expensive.

'It takes commitment and discipline,' I said, meeting Jay's grey-blue eyes, the colour of Port Phillip Bay when the sun refused to shine. 'It means remembering where your priorities are. Isaac and I started this thing because we want to stay together forever and make it work.'

'"Commitment and discipline". What does that even mean?' asked Jay. 'Do you fuck without emotion?' He smiled a challenge at me. 'I can't imagine you doing that. You're … quite intense.'

'I know. Too intense. But that's how it's supposed to work, according to Isaac.' I took my teaspoon and played with the froth on my latte. 'Isaac's a rationalist. He lives mostly in his head – that's part of our problem. But for me, what's the point of fucking without emotion?' My voice was getting louder as I warmed to my complaint. 'There's no separation in me. Heart, mind, cunt – where's the divide?' The women at the table next door stopped mid-sentence and looked over at me; they'd heard 'cunt' as a curse. 'No doubt they call theirs pussies or lady gardens,' I said to Jay. 'And when they visit their gynies, they get technical and call them *vaginas*.' I hoped they'd hear.

Jay laughed at me, reaching for my hands across the table. 'Come, sweetheart, let's go.'

Later, when I said to him, in the midst of joyful, eyes wide open, hard and tender fucking, 'I was made for this', he replied without question, 'This is where I want to be.' It was whispered into my ear from behind, so quietly it was more of a vibration on my earlobe than a sound.

We giggled at the corny language of love, the point where good taste departed and feelings gave rise to words that were ridiculous but still true in the moment.

Grinding slowly, eye to eye, belly to belly, with a slit of golden light coming in through his curtains, I said, 'Nothing is as good as this.' And we both knew that what I meant was the meld of love and fucking. Falling, falling. We were going there fast.

Afterwards, staring up at the high moulded ceiling of his cool dark bedroom, I reminded myself, 'I'll never leave Isaac', saying it as a hopeful declaration.

'I'm depending on it,' Jay said grimly, and I didn't understand. 'Tell me,' he said, 'do I have permission to fall in love with you anyway?'

'Of course.'

I had no idea what I was doing or where I was heading, except that this was too delicious and I wanted more. Whether or not it was against the rules.

~⌒~

Jay and I wake up in Perth after a hectic night of trying to sleep together for the first time. After several months of afternoon sex in his beautiful bed in St Kilda, with its 600-thread Egyptian cotton sheets, we've never actually slept, apart from a trickly doze; never woken up beside each other.

The day is too grey and cold for the beach, so Esther suggests the three of us go into the city, to King Street for a coffee and some clothes shopping.

Jay struggles with the morning. He's a night owl and I can see his alternate clock ticking away all over his crumpled face, telling him he should be back in bed and not even thinking about breakfast until 3pm, Melbourne time. I laugh at him without compassion. I don't believe him when he says he's nocturnal; that even before he was a theatre critic with overnight deadlines, when he used to hold down a day job, he was a struggling zombie. I don't buy that story, instead thinking that he's soft and self-indulgent and looking for attention. He should learn to cope, or twist himself back into the patterns of waking and sleeping that ordinary people follow. He is wilfully abnormal.

We find a cafe in a narrow cobbled lane, and sit down at a table deep inside the wood-panelled cavern. Jay orders eggs Benedict and a strong flat white. Esther and I pick at a shared bowl of fresh fruit salad and pour ourselves cups of milky tea. We watch with serious, longing eyes as Jay pierces the egg yolks and sops up the vivid yellow flow with a piece of English muffin; part of us longs to be eating that creamy mess but we won't ingest the calories. On our own, we watch our weight, but when we're together we eat even less, competing silently and taking strength from each other's self-denial. Right now, we're surviving on one meal a day – usually a rich and satisfying dinner. Our bellies are flat and our hips narrow. My size eight skirts are starting to hang off me. I like it.

Jay doesn't care about calories, or about cholesterol, for that matter. He lets his belly grow large and round, like a big, furry, friendly egg. And his regular diet consists of so many eggs, and so much milk and toast and orange juice, that I can only wonder what nursery meals he missed out on as a child. Or is it always breakfast in a world where you wake as the sun goes down?

He takes a sip of his coffee and his happy, hungry face turns cold. Petulant, I think. He gestures for the waitress and sends the coffee back. 'It's pissweak,' he says with a steely smile.

And so the coffees come out, and are sent back, one by one. The second is still too weak, the next is too cold; there's one that's slopped on the saucer. The poor young waitress, wearing too much eyeliner and with a jangle of earrings dangling beside her innocent, pimpled face, blushes as she puts down the final coffee. She's probably never encountered such an un-malicious but harsh critic before.

Esther and I smile at her with sympathetic embarrassment. All of a sudden I long for Isaac, with his gentle, unfastidious ways. He would look at such a girl, and drink the cold, weak slopped offerings she put before him, partly because he wouldn't care too much about such things, and partly because he would feel sweet pity for her. Darling man. I miss his voice.

So I take my mobile phone out into the street and call my husband. He's at work, and I can hear the background hum of his office: the tapping keyboards, the ringing phones, the printers spewing out project management directives. He's deep in that cave where he creates long chains of the programming language he loves, but he's pleased to talk to me, and we slip into our silly, mundane banter. I ask him what he's going to have for lunch and he asks me what I've had for breakfast, and if I'm eating enough; he doesn't want me to be a skeleton by the time he arrives. We don't mention Jay. Isaac knows Jay is here, and I know he knows, but there isn't any need to bring him up.

We finish with the love talk that is like a prayer, worn out but still beautiful, trying desperately to be truthful in its essence.

'I love you,' I say.

'I'll love you forever.'

'You hang up.'

'No, you hang up.'

'You're still there.'

'Bye-bye, darling.'

'Hey …?' I ask.

But Isaac's gone, and the phone is warm against my ear, a quickly cooling corpse.

Now breakfast is finished and we're out shopping. Esther and I talk about how we need new bathers, but we look over at Jay and think this might be stretching his tolerance for girly stuff.

How little we know him. 'Come on, let's look at swimsuits! Let's find you the perfect pair.'

'But we don't know if we want you to see us trying them on,' says Esther timidly.

'It's so intimate,' I add. 'More intimate than oral sex, and much more painful.'

Of course the mention of oral sex makes Jay want to look at bathers even more, as if it's some kinky activity he can add to his repertoire, a story he can make of this excruciating female activity. He will be so proud of the access he's been granted.

We find a store that's full of scraps of lycra, with smoky mirrors and flattering lights and thick flesh-coloured carpet that makes us want to sit down on it and rest. The salesgirl smiles at us as we walk in, but she doesn't get off the phone. I can see by her glance that she thinks Jay's our 'girlfriend', a safe gay aesthete brought along for judgement and good humour. It's a mistake that's made all the time, and Jay bears it with grim patience, secure in his much-tried heterosexuality. Only occasionally does he bristle, when he's excluded from macho conversations, or when the point is pressed as it sometimes is: 'You must be gay. You *must* be. You just don't know it.'

For now, though, he's happy to own the shop. He walks along the racks, picking out a selection for us to try. Esther guides him away from the tinier bikinis and I tell him to put back the white swimsuits that go see-through when wet. He nods, taking direction seriously, and apart from these lapses, his intuition is surprisingly good. Esther parades in a hot-pink halter-neck bikini, and I think she looks like the perfect fifties bubblegum princess, blonde and fun and effervescent. But Jay bites his lip and puts his head to the side, and says, 'No, you can do better.'

He hands her a strange black one-piece that's cut out at the sides, a tiny and complicated bit of corsetry. When Esther emerges from behind the curtain, after much fiddling with what goes where, she's a seventies Helmut Newton sophisticate, her small perfect breasts separated by a deep-cut V. Her legs seem to go on forever, even without the silly high heels this style suggests.

Jay lets out a sigh. 'Perfect.' And he's right. Esther won't buy it, though. It's just for fun.

But I'm a serious shopper, and now I trust him to find me something. At first I'm insulted that he'd even think to put me in modest and prosaic Speedos – boring, corporate, navy blue, the colour of school uniforms! But when I see what he sees, I understand. He has me looking like a sleek, dark swimming creature, bottom firmly contained, breasts up high and round, and the muscles in my arms and shoulders long, strong and brown. As if I could swim forever.

'Sexy-as,' he says.

I bow to his verdict, submit to him, and tell him that it's no wonder people pay him for his taste. He grabs me and pushes down a navy shoulder strap, kissing my skin hard as if he's going to bite it. The salesgirl raises her eyebrows, revising assumptions. I shut my eyes and I think that here is a man who sees me, objectifies me, desires me. And he knows me.

We wake late the next day, and the sun is high in the sky by the time we rise from morning sex. I'm sore and itchy from too much of it; the doctor will wonder if it's 'honeymoon cystitis' when I visit later that week. But now the beach calls, and even if the breeze feels too stiff already, Jay insists that today is the day. He's on holiday and he's come here with my promise of white sand, blue waves and the idea of lying in the sun beside me. I must give it to him.

Jay doesn't own bathers, swimmers, boardies or budgie-smugglers. He tells me this in the bedroom as I pack my new Speedos in a canvas bag, along with some old sun-crunchy beach towels from Esther's linen cupboard and a battered straw hat I found on the back porch. I stop and look at him. He's sitting there, ready to leave, with just a book and some sunscreen in his hands.

'Seriously,' I say, 'you have nothing to swim in?'

'My last pair must have been back in the early eighties. I don't see the point.'

'So what do you do when you go to the swimming pool, or hang out with friends at the beach?'

'I don't go to swimming pools. I'd rather swim in a urinal.' He wrinkles his nose. 'And I only go to the beach with very good friends. Beaches where clothing is optional.'

'Nude beaches! You're a nudist?'

'A naturist, darling.'

'So I guess we have to go to Swanbourne then?' I ask warily.

I've heard of the famous nude beach in jokes about paedophiles and perverts and their wobbly-jelly games of volleyball. Then there are the jokes about firing and shots, and loaded guns, because the dunes of Swanbourne front an army training barracks and its practice shooting range.

'Yes, please, take me there,' he says imperiously. 'I've been wanting to check it out for ages.'

'And what about me? Can I wear my clothes?'

'Darling, you can do what you want, whatever you're comfortable with. But I think you'll love it. You're an exhibitionist, you just don't know it yet.'

'Is that why you do it, because you're an exhibitionist?'

'No,' he says with a smile, 'but you are.'

'We'll see.' I spread sunscreen all over my naked body, just in case, and also because I know that it's best to do this before you're battling the sandy wind on location. I put on my bra and undies, and a cotton sundress over the top.

Jay tells me he's a connoisseur of nude or 'free' beaches around Australia. He wants to compare Swanbourne with his favourite, Maslin in South Australia. 'Did you know that Maslin is the only free beach that was opened by a state premier? Don Dunstan, in '75. Bless his little pink shorts!' He takes such delight in facts like these.

'Really?' I ask. 'There was an actual ribbon to cut for a nude beach?'

'Look it up. I'm old enough to remember it.' He grins and doesn't look very old at all.

In 1975 I was a toddler, already singing love songs to Jesus with the New Guinea people, and learning about sin, the wages of it being death. My beautiful young parents, so very young – the age I am right at this minute – were missionaries and visionaries, the spirit of the seventies manifested in them by evangelical zeal. They were working towards the imminent day of God's return.

I wanted to wear a bikini, even as a toddler on those Pacific sands. I remember asking for one; I must've been five or six then, in Port Moresby, as I watched the other Australian expats frolicking nearly naked in the warm shallows. Diplomats, adventurers, tourists – they certainly weren't there to 'convert the natives'. Smokers and drinkers and sun worshippers all of them, they seemed more foreign to me than the brown, skinny children I played with, and the dark men speaking Pidgin English with my father as they paddled his canoe to the outer islands for prayer meetings. I caught sight of a little girl in a bikini and wanted one just like it, two sleek triangles on top and one at the bottom, leaving her tanned belly free to feel the sun and the waves. My mother shook her head gently as she looked over at the party under a nearby coconut tree. The tangy heathen scent of barbecuing meat wafted in our direction, along with laughter fuelled by eskies of local beer. 'We're not like that, darling. They're non-Adventists.'

~

I'm at the steering wheel and Jay sits beside me, his hand on my thigh. We're driving along the coast, heading north from Cottesloe – the beach Esther, Claudia and I would ordinarily visit because we love its safety. We feel secure with the lifeguards on shark-watch, the crowds of many-shaped bodies on show, and the mothers with small children who keep things gentle on the shoreline. We like the huge old Norfolk pines up near the road and the lawn underneath, a shady picnic place away from the sand. Whenever we go to Cottesloe, Claudia stays under those trees in billowy shorts and a big hat, reading

Jane Austen and protecting her complexion, while Esther and I swim out as deep as we dare.

Jay and I are heading towards the wilder beaches, where there's no shelter from the wind or the sun. We're wearing sunglasses; when we smile at each other, our eyes are hidden beneath blank mirrors smiling back at us. The windows are down and a hot breeze whooshes through the car, mingling with and diffusing our music. It's Fleetwood Mac's *Greatest Hits*, the old warped cassette that Esther never removes from her car's tape deck. The music lives on and on, despite the buckling heat.

Jay and I sing along joyously with 'Little Lies', out of tune deliberately to mask our mistakes. He's crooning to me and I'm doing the echo, and I'm wondering if he actually needs me to tell him lies. We've talked about my honesty in the past, and the way it's the golden virtue I held fast to when I left the Church. But what about now?

'Did you ever see the video clip for this song?' he asks, winding up the window. 'It's so bad, it's good. They're at this farmyard, and Stevie's dressed up like a granny in a floaty white dress –'

'Do you ever lie?' I ask suddenly, winding up my window to match his.

'I try not to,' he says. 'We all do sometimes. But I know you tell me what I need to know.' He squeezes my thigh playfully. 'I rely on it.'

'You think I tell you the truth all the time?'

'You're an open book,' he says arrogantly. 'I'd feel it if you were lying to me.'

'You're so cocky.' I wish he suspected me more, because that would make me feel less alone, more understood. 'You'd better be careful.'

He's quiet now, and I can feel him blowing away from me, distant.

'What's wrong?' I ask. 'Did I offend you?'

'Not at all,' he says a little coldly. 'I'm three days behind with The Diary – I must make some notes before I go to bed tonight.'

I look at him to see if he's serious. Does he have any idea how ridiculously pompous he sounds? 'I can't believe you're worrying about your *diary*. As if there are some rules about keeping it every single day. You're on holiday!'

'I do keep it every single day,' he retorts. 'Even if it's just a few words to jolt the memory so I can fill in the blanks later.' His mouth is hard and sulky now. 'It bothers me to lose the thread.'

'What are you, fourteen?' I try to soften the insult with a cheeky grin, but he doesn't see it. Do I really think he's foolish, rigid, weird – or am I just baiting him?

'It's something I like to do.'

'You know I love your diary, especially when I'm in it! But there are limits. How long has this been going on, like twenty years?'

'More than twenty. I know exactly how long, to the day, but you'll mock me if I tell you.'

'Sorry. Don't you think it's a bit … extreme?' I'm goading him now, and I can't stop.

'It's a task I've set myself, Eve.' He says my name very precisely. Stubborn.

'So are you going to publish it? Do you think you're the next Proust?'

'It's for me. It doesn't need to make sense to you.'

'I just don't see why you have to take it so seriously.'

'You'd do well to take your own writing more seriously.'
His face is grave and angry. I look at him and then stare straight
ahead at the road. He's daggered me where it hurts, the tender
place where I know what I should be doing – writing – but am
not brave enough.

Our letters to each other have become the word-stitched
backbone of this odd new creature we're creating, the couple
that is 'us'. Days after our first afternoon in bed, we exchanged
email addresses and the writing began: the elated discovery of
each other in another dimension.

His emails are sent in the early hours of the morning, after
he has filed his copy for work. I collect them with my noisy,
ker-plunking dial-up modem as soon as I wake, when Isaac has
gone off to work. Jay sends snatches of The Diary – pieces he
feels are 'fit for human consumption', paragraphs that relate to
the discussions we've been having about art and love and the
nature of intimacy. There are descriptions, clinical almost, of
my body and the sex we have. There are reviews too, pieces
about theatre and dance and opera.

I read it all carefully, searching for clues to his public
persona, things I might need to know before I reveal my
own writing and my own fledgling intellect. Then I spend an
hour or two, every morning, crafting a response, still wearing
pyjamas and drinking coffee, with my fat Persian cat, Lulu, on
my lap. This is the luxury of the PhD student who should be
writing a thesis but is instead writing herself a love story. The
ultimate procrastination.

My letters are careful and beautiful at first – I'm fully aware of Jay's pedantry for grammar and spelling – and braver as they go on. Memories of childhood inspired by the floral, febrile excess of DH Lawrence, because Jay has got me reading *The Rainbow* and I fully embrace its style. There are pieces of my own haphazard diary and tentative explanations for why I am what I am: an unfaithful wife who cannot leave; a terrible cynic but an addict for love; a hedonist ('A sybarite, darling,' Jay says); and a backslidden Christian who no longer believes in Heaven but still thinks she's going to Hell – or the Adventist version of it.

I'm searching for my voice and finding it, becoming fearlessly candid under Jay's gaze, which is critical but always accepting. He loves my honesty, tells me it's rare. There's no praise when he thinks I deserve none, and he has surprising admiration for things I didn't know I possessed. And he tells me, almost straight away, that I'm a writer and that writing is the other thing I'm made for.

But I'm afraid. Proud and afraid, and not sure what to do with this information. To be published for writing about the things that mean anything to me – cinema, sex, love and transgression – is unthinkable, a mountain too high to climb. And if I were to be published, I'd break my parents' hearts. I am ashamed, for so many reasons.

'Touché,' I say in the car, finally. 'I should be more serious about my writing.'

I feel Jay's warm hand on my thigh again, forgiving me. He hasn't told me he loves me since he landed in Perth three days ago, but there's this – skin on skin – and it's enough for now.

So this is Swanbourne. We've made our way through the high dunes, following the sandy corridor that forms a natural walkway between them. The beach stretches out in front of us, that huge extravagant expanse of white sand that West Australians take for granted. It's midday on a weekday, and the sea breeze has well and truly set in for the afternoon. Only the determined – the tourists, or the lovers – would bother with a day like this when there are so many others to choose from. In the distance are two people in the rough surf – naked, no doubt, but submerged. A man and a woman?

We make camp high up the beach, far away from the water where the dunes begin, finding a natural hollow that's sheltered from the wind. Tufts of yellow-green sea grass sprout from the sides of our laid-out towels. I sit there fully clothed while Jay strips, folding his clothes neatly as he goes. Shirt, trousers, boxers. There he is now, naked except for a cap. He sits on his towel, knees bent, belly against thighs, spreading a dot of sunscreen sparingly over his face.

'Want me to do your back?' I ask.

'No, I think I'll get a tan for a while.'

'You'll burn in ten minutes.' I grab the sunscreen from him and kneel behind his back like a bossy mother, spreading dollops over his freckled shoulders.

He shrugs away from me. 'Not too much! I want to let some sun through.'

'You're from a different generation, the one before the hole in the ozone layer. You're careless about prophylaxis of all kinds!'

He lets out a short whooping laugh and grabs the sunscreen from me, spreading it down his long legs and back up again.

'Don't forget your cock,' I say with a smirk.

'I did it before we left home. I'd never be caught dead applying sunscreen to my dick.'

'Isn't that par for the course on a nude beach?'

'No, there's etiquette. That's very bad form, unless you're a pervert. Looks too much like wanking. And if you do get an erection, best lie on your stomach and burrow into the sand.' He grins at me. 'You girls have it easy.'

Then he goes ahead and lies down on his stomach, though he's clearly not aroused. His face is turned away from me, and he gives a great satisfied sigh as the sun beats down on his round winter-pale arse, narrow and high and innocently plump like a baby's. The back of him is so much younger than the front.

I look down at the green sea, the white-capped waves crashing in hypnotically. I raise my nose to the breeze. The salty smell of freedom. And I know, as I knew before, that yes, I will take off my clothes and present myself, all of myself, to the sun.

The sun, the sun, it's always been my first love, the source of private ecstasies. I remember my first surprising orgasm at the age of seven. Dressed in bathers, I was leaning against the side of our aqua-coloured above-ground swimming pool, facing the dense Fijian bush at the back of our house, the sun beating down on me and a black fly crawling up my inner thigh towards my crotch, where my fingers were jammed inside. All nature combined in one hot and humid moment that made me cry out. Then came the shame when I was caught, something I can hardly remember because it's too terrible.

Now I strip quickly, businesslike. Jay pretends not to notice – as if his glance might scare me off. I lie on my back,

hat covering my face completely; it's quiet under there, a
retreat. There's only sensation now. The smell of sunscreen
and hot straw, and the sound of my breath. Thoughts stop.
The breeze tickles my nipples and teases the dark triangle
of hair I have come to accept but never love. I can feel the
sun there now, as though this is the only part of my body it's
interested in, its rays burrowing in where it has never been
before, not even for an instant.

~⌀

The week flies fast, with Jay and me and Esther, and sometimes
Claudia, making meals, going out to parties, taking trips to
the bottle shop, the beach, the movies. And after the beautiful
warm days filled with talk and laughter, Jay and I shut the door
and go off to bed, where we spend hours testing the limits of
each other's endurance. I start to fade at midnight, but for him
it's the middle of the day, and he pushes me past my weariness
until I'm dizzy and nearly fainting, almost delirious.

He keeps stroking my body with that firm, sure touch I find
irresistible. The ambiguity of that touch is part of its magic; I'm
never sure if his strokes are friendly or lustful. The intentions of
his hands are unclear, opaque, unthreatening, but I find myself
determined to clarify those intentions, to turn those sensuous
strokes into full-blown fucking – to test him until I'm sure he
desires me. I want the definitive fuck that will prove to me that
he wants me and won't say no to me, the way Isaac does.

Of course it's not enough that Jay wants me, which he
obviously does, sometimes five times a day. I need him to love
me, and he still hasn't said it in Perth. Why was it so easy for

him to say it back in Melbourne, and why is he withholding it now? It's making me angry and needy.

'I love you,' I tell him, one hot dark night when we're both drenched with sweat, and the blue light of dawn is driving me into dangerous territory.

'Thank you,' he says, pulling himself out of me, his still slick cock wilting in its condom after the last round.

'Why don't you say it back?' I pull my leg up carefully and turn over, away from him.

'Did you tell me you loved me because you felt it, or because you wanted to hear me say it?'

I'm angry at his insight. 'Is it wrong for me to want that?'

'It's wrong for me to say it if I don't want to. I've told you so many times before that I love you. But saying it has to feel right, in that moment.'

'And why doesn't it feel right, in this moment – or *any* moment, since you got here?'

'I don't know,' he says, 'maybe it's because you feel … shallower here. What we have doesn't seem to matter so much to you.' He rolls off the condom, wrapping it into a ball of tissue and throwing it across the room, where it lands perfectly in the wastepaper basket beside the dresser. I think of Marcus and the way he did the same thing, just a week ago.

'Shallower?' I ask, feeling insulted. 'I'm on holiday. You want me to be *deeper*?'

'I don't know. I just feel as though I can't quite trust you here.'

Is he onto me, I wonder? What does he feel with those sensors of his, that intuition that perceives different bands on the spectrum?

'Love is an action and a decision, not just a feeling,' I say, remembering the premarital counselling Isaac and I had with the pastor at church: the discussions of love and commitment and how you needed to stay together even when the feelings weren't there, because if you said it enough, and believed it enough, they would return.

'Does that mean you've said it to me when you weren't really feeling it?' asks Jay.

'I guess so, but it was still true.'

The truth is I've forgotten – if I ever knew – how to differentiate the feeling of love, in the moment, from my own need, or from history, or from a shared narrative where the repetition of those words is part of a doctrine. And even here, with my lover who owes me nothing and has made no vows, I want the surety and the promise.

'It makes me feel so rejected that you haven't felt good enough "in the moment" the whole time you've been here, to be able to say it to me,' I tell Jay sulkily.

'I'll never say no to you sexually,' he assures me, stroking the small of my back. 'That's a kind of love I thought you'd recognise.'

'You're saying that you'd fuck me even if you didn't feel like it, in the moment?'

'It wouldn't take me long to get myself in the mood. And that's what you need from me.'

'And yet telling me you love me if you're not quite feeling it that very second is faking it?'

'It's a subtle thing. It has to feel right.' His tricky, evasive logic makes me angry.

'You think you know me so well, and that you understand

exactly what I need, but you know nothing.' I sit up in bed with the pale blue sheet pulled high over my breasts.

Suddenly I want to show him what he doesn't know. I want him to know the truth of what I am, what I've done. My weak betraying heart and body. My confusion. I want him to discard me now if he needs to, or else to swallow me whole and love me – to tell me he loves me – in spite of it.

So I tell him the truth.

I tell him about the rough marital fuck that Isaac insisted upon – as an act of possession? – before he took me to the airport the night I left Melbourne. I tell him about seeing Marcus again, that echo-chamber of memories and feelings, an old song to be replayed for nostalgia's sake and for the power of overturning the failure all those years ago. And finally, I tell him about Peter, and that floating conquest – by me, or by Peter, I'm not really sure.

Jay lies there, looking up at me as I talk. He strokes my nearest thigh without faltering, as if he's enjoying the feel of the muscle there. His calmness is unnerving. I want him to cry, or slap me, or turn away in disgust. But he just gazes at me as if nothing's changed, making small noises of sympathy – is he *sorry* for me? He asks questions that seem entirely irrelevant: 'Has Isaac apologised yet?' or 'What was it like to fuck Marcus again? As good as you remembered?' He even cracks the occasional joke: 'So did you ever get that coffee from Peter or was it just a ruse?'

Instead of being grateful for Jay's calm reception of the news, I turn angry, accusing him of coldness. If he cared for me at all, if he loved me as he says he does – or did – then why won't he punish me for my misdeeds? Why won't he be jealous?

'Don't you care if I screw around?' I ask, kicking him away with a knee to his chest.

Now he turns his bare freckled back to me. I'm sitting up against the pillows and looking at his long, pale body, the body that's given me so much pleasure, so generously; a body that seems part of my own this week, and almost repulsive because of that.

I put my hand on his shoulder and he shrugs it off. 'Don't touch me right now. I'm appalled by your lack of faith.'

'I don't understand.'

He turns over onto his back without looking at me and says to the ceiling, 'You told me what you'd done and I accepted it. And now I'm being punished for – what? Hearing you?'

I'm silent for a long time, wondering at this alien creature whose responses are so different from my own. 'But doesn't it matter to you what I've done?'

'Of course it matters. But I understand. I know what it's like to be out of control.'

'You think I'm out of control?'

'Maybe … yes,' he admits. 'I've been there myself. A while ago I fucked three women in forty-eight hours.' I think for a moment that I hate him because he might be proud of it. But he continues, and I don't think he's bragging after all. 'I had a girlfriend and I started having an affair. Then I ended up cheating on both of them.' He pauses, and I can't help wondering if he'll cheat on me. The idea is a kick in my guts. I couldn't stand it. I know how hypocritical this is. 'Once you've betrayed someone you love,' he continues softly, 'it's just a matter of degree. It's easy to spin out of control. And you can hate yourself afterwards. But I don't hate you. I just want to understand you.'

'Doesn't it change how you feel about me?' I ask shyly.

'Having you all to myself was never part of the picture,' he says. 'You make that very clear to me whenever you tell me you'll never leave Isaac. I live with that. You're able to love more than one person – it's the way you're built and one of the things I find interesting about you.'

'Yes,' I say. 'But this is different.'

'It only matters if it makes you treat me badly. And it only matters if it changes how you feel about me.' He's silent, waiting for me to digest it all. Then he asks, '*Does* it change how you feel about me?'

'No.'

I realise that I care more about him now than I ever have.

'I'm a bitch,' I say, sliding down so our faces are close on the pillow.

'Yes. Yes, you are.' He kisses me softly for a very long time.

～♡

It's a cool grey dawn and I'm at the airport putting Jay on a plane back to Melbourne. Tonight, he will have a drink with Isaac in St Kilda – 'pass the baton', as they joke. They'll never be friends but it seems to be some code of honour between them that they stay in touch, and every so often share a beer and demonstrate to the world that they have no rancour. Tomorrow, Isaac will be on a plane to the west.

For a moment I long for the simplicity of loving one person at a time. An imagined simplicity, I remind myself.

But now, I kiss Jay as if I'll die with the loss of him. We feel so close. I can hardly bear to count how many days there are until I return to his bed in Melbourne. And then, at the departure gate, I panic because I'm saying goodbye to the only man in the world who knows the full truth. 'I don't want you to go!' I say.

He holds me tightly, then hands me a gift of poetry: Rilke. 'You're the right age for this now. It's a young person's book. But a good one.' He pulls me close for another long hug. 'I love you,' he says into my ear before turning and leaving, too quickly for me to say it back. It doesn't matter. He knows I do.

I take the book home to Esther's with me, into bed with the dawn, and lie there reading about the inchoate longings of angels.

9

Esther and I clean the house with frantic zeal, ruining our fingernails and spoiling our t-shirts with violent splashes of bleach. We even take care of the small details, poking around the taps with a toothbrush, polishing the mirrors, and vacuuming away the spiders from behind wardrobes and bookshelves. I wonder why we feel the need to have the place sparkling for Isaac. He's a dreamy slob and couldn't care less as long as he has a comfortable bed and a good reading light. Why are we so afraid to let him see our dirt?

But we don't ask any questions or discuss our purpose. We don't even consciously divide up the tasks. We simply dance the dance, and we're old partners, elegant and easy, performing a ritual that we only vaguely understand. We move from room to room, from downstairs to upstairs, until the whole house is immaculate. Then we spill out into the garden, pulling weeds and sweeping pavement.

Esther finds an ant nest and sets about stirring it up with a stick. Fetching a can from inside, she sprays at the black stream of ants pouring out of the tiny volcano. She's absorbed, squatting with her thighs apart and her bare feet planted firmly in the dirt. Sweat beads on the fine blonde hairs above her lip. I'm reminded of the busy, intense little girl she used to be, her cheeks pink with exertion as she kept her focus long after other children had abandoned the playground, or the pool, or the Nintendo.

Since we were children, Esther and I have known how to lose ourselves in hard-working games that evolve hour by hour. Perhaps this cleaning madness is just another game. It's not always friendly and sometimes mean thoughts and short words flash through the air with the flying dust or grass. But these minor hostilities never survive the blast of our shared humour and history. Outside of my family, she is the first one who taught me what it is to love someone, and live beside them, through waves of irritation and boredom, waiting for the good times to return. Holding on.

Looking at Esther right now, I feel a pang of disdain for her. Why kill the ants? Why now? It's a pointless task and she's wasting time. But I go inside and bring out a hat and a cold drink for her, and she looks up at me with a guilty, apologetic wince.

'I hate, hate, *hate* them,' she says, stomping on another ant.

'I know, but you've got most of them, and there's always tomorrow.' I take the spray can gently out of her hand, the way you might take a gun from a child, and pull her to her feet. She relents, because we're a team of two, united and inseparable.

This is why we're anxious, I realise. We're preparing for the ultimate intruder, the one person who thinks he has the inalienable right to come between us. My husband. He doesn't like it, the way Esther and I laugh at unspoken jokes.

The bickering undercurrents that absorb us but dissolve into nothing; the memories that unspool in tangled silky stories that catch us up for hours at a time. We exclude others without even trying, as if they exist merely as an audience for our intimacy.

Isaac hasn't liked it on the brief holidays we've taken together, and he didn't like it when Esther spent the first few days of our married life poking her head in the door and stealing me for sightseeing expeditions around Melbourne. I feel tense remembering these times. Isaac didn't want a honeymoon – but he didn't want my best friend along for the first days of his married life either.

Now it's time to get ready for the airport. We shower and dress quietly, without the usual noise of the radio. There's something earnest and ceremonial about Esther as she comes into my bedroom and asks me what I'm going to wear. I've laid out the simplest thing I can find: a small white dress with a collar and no sleeves. It reminds me of purity and coolness, of nuns and nurses and prim little tennis players. Or sixties miniskirted brides. I slip the dress on and brush my hair, fold a yellow scarf into a headband.

'You look like a frangipani,' says Esther, who knows they're my favourite flower. She looks like a garden herself, in an explosion of vintage floral tat that comes right out of her mother's seventies ragbag. She's wearing the blue crystal drop-earrings that make tiny rainbows on her cheeks when she moves her head in the sunlight. The earrings she wore when I met her.

'I feel nervous,' I say. 'I'm afraid –'

'Shh. It'll be fine. Just remember, it's Isaac, the man you love best in the entire world.' Esther takes my hand and leads me out the door, pushing me in front of her. She may as well be pushing me down the aisle and shoving a bouquet in my hand. I look at her face as she stares straight ahead, and I can tell that she's trying as hard as she can to do the right thing, say the right thing, support me in the vows she knows I can't break without breaking myself up into a thousand pieces.

～

When Isaac comes through the arrivals gate, Esther and I watch him for a little while before he sees us. I like looking at him as if he's a stranger, trying to imagine what I might see if he weren't my husband. He's big. He's tall, standing a head higher than most of the other passengers. It's like he's descended from some far-eastern European race of towering, fine people with broad cheekbones and Slavic slanted eyes, heavy-lidded, lazy-looking but quick behind his round, wire-rimmed glasses.

He looks like a reluctant predator. His chin-length hair is a black rock-star mess. He's ugly and he's beautiful all in one androgynous confusion – is he a horrible woman or a too-pretty man? I call him my wonderful creature, because he's so singular, monstrous and divine. He's wearing a shirt of acid-green synthetic fibres that clings to his chest. He's been spending time in the gym this year, pumping weights as if our marriage depended upon it, and perhaps I suggested that it did, when I told him I *needed* him to exercise because he was getting heavy.

I remember when I first met him and he had a flat, narrow chest like a young girl's. He wasn't fully grown then. I loved the boyish smoothness of his unfallen body with its tiny half-formed nipples and the violet appendectomy scar just below the hip bone. I liked the way his small, round bum-cheeks sat atop those long, almost hairless legs – legs I envied for their slender perfection.

What a crime to marry a man still in the teenage chrysalis, a man who has never known another woman. He was twenty when I met him, one year older than me, but still a virgin, a boy without a driver's licence. I drove him round until he passed his test, and then he had to put the P-plates up for the first year of our marriage. A hassle for me to take them down whenever I got behind the wheel.

He sees us now, and his voice calls out, 'Hello, hello!' theatrical and loud as if he's on a stage projecting his presence to an indifferent audience. He looks pale and a little thinner than when I last saw him. He comes over and I see the fear shadowing his smile as he reaches for me and kisses me full on the lips for longer than I'm comfortable with in public.

I think of Esther standing witness and I pull away. He hugs her too, tells her she looks fabulous, then turns to me: 'Doesn't she look fabulous, Eve?'

'Yes, Isaac, she looks fabulous.'

'She's as pretty as a flower – and so, my little darling dear, are you. All in white like the day I married you. God, you're getting brown, though. Too much sun.' He grabs the back of my skirt and hitches it up so he can see my thighs. I wriggle away, embarrassed. But he keeps teasing. 'Far too much sizzling sun and you'll be a shrunken, shrivelled lily-flower. But never mind, my sister, my bride, "All beautiful you are, my darling. There is no flaw in you."'

He's quoting the Song of Solomon, mixed up with his own camp shtick. Esther looks at me and raises an eyebrow. *Shut up and drop the performing monkey act*, is what she's thinking.

I feel sorry for Isaac and see him pitiful under her gaze. But he's sweet too, as he draws me close to him and bends his head down to take a private sniff of my hair, staying quiet for a moment as if the scent might revive his failing energy.

We start to walk, Isaac in the middle with one arm around Esther and one around me. Now he's prattling about the flight, about the Stanisław Lem novel he's been reading, about the horrible weather he left behind and the 'dastardly clever' code he's been writing at work. I want to tell him to be quiet, to stop and breathe the air for a minute, to look me in the eye and answer the mundane little questions I want to ask, the ones that connect me back to our life together. Like, how much money do we have left in the bank till next payday? And what the hell has he been eating to make him look so pale and sickly?

But I lacquer a smile to my face and hold my silence. I remember advice I've been given about my lashing serpent's tongue; a 'viper', my mother sometimes called me when we argued, invoking the Old Testament Proverbs. She wondered if I'd ever find a husband – the worst fate in the world being that I wouldn't – and if I did, she predicted with fury, I'd destroy him with my words. I took those insults deep into my teenage heart, even while I screamed at her.

Right now, all I want to do is criticise, to pick and pull at Isaac, to make him into a perfect reflection of myself – or someone much better and more polished, so I can love him more. I want to smooth out the creases in his clothes (badly ironed, I notice, because it's usually me who does his shirts), erase the gaucheness from his conversation, the show-off flourishes that reveal he's trying too hard. I want to squeeze the blackheads on his nose, brush the hair out of his eyes.

Isaac has become a relative, a family member, and so sometimes he is unbearable.

We're wheeling his suitcase out of the airport into the car park. He squints in the bright sunshine; already his hair is turning sweaty and clinging in tendrils around his white forehead. He's such an outsider in this land of sand and sun and scrappy trees. He reminds me of a vampire dragged out into the daylight. He belongs in the gloom of old buildings huddled against dramatic wind or endless drizzle; in libraries, cinemas and universities; on trams and trains, or striding through solemn green parks in overcoats and clomping heavy shoes. Yes, he belongs under an umbrella, in Melbourne. I almost laugh at the idea of taking him to the beach. Whatever shall we do here for the next week?

I let Isaac sit next to Esther up front, and I climb into the back, leaning against the cushioned helplessness of childhood. Sunglasses on, I watch the scrubby deadness as we drive past ugly roads and belching trucks, and see what Isaac must be seeing on his first visit to Perth. My home town at its ugliest: hot, dry and bleak.

It's as if he can read my mind. 'Beautiful city, Eve. I can see why you miss it.'

'You haven't even seen it yet,' I say, thinking that this ugliness is not so different from the suburb where we live in Melbourne.

'I think I've seen enough. I want to go home.' He winks at Esther. He loves pressing these buttons. But there's something in the way he holds his shoulders that lets me know he's not going to submit to my city, no matter how the river might sparkle or the white beaches stretch out into stupidly beautiful imitations of postcards. It's not his beloved Melbourne.

He's always been heartless about my homesickness, and won't hear a word of criticism against the city that's his natural habitat. It makes him cross when I scorn Melbourne's weather or bemoan the tram-tracks that turn the traffic into higgledy chaos, or dare to point out that the Yarra is a shitty little toxic river compared to the Swan, and that pathetic bayside beaches aren't worth the sand in my crotch. So I voice these criticisms whenever I'm feeling mean and helpless and trapped.

Might there be other places worth living in the world? In Australia even? Never. Isaac won't move on this question, or from the barren outer flat-brick suburbs where we've found ourselves lately, having outgrown the need to be near his uni. How I hate living there, with the long drives inwards and outwards, with each homecoming journey feeling like a sad departure. I want to live with my likeminded friends in the beating heart of the city, with streets that ooze late into the night with talk and drink, and the low rumble of ideas waiting to be born in early morning epiphanies. So I imagine.

The irony is that Isaac was one such romantic urban creature when we met, with his boyish bedroom window looking down on one of the busiest streets in the city, and his childhood etched into the back alleys of Carlton, his playground the Queen Vic Market and the gardens of Melbourne University where his father kept a tutor's flat. Perhaps that's why Isaac doesn't need it now, why he feels that moving so far out into the suburbs is a means of getting away from his parents.

He tells me I'm an inner-city snob as I decry the concrete ugliness of Italianate mansions; the mushrooming satellite dishes on acres of red-tile roofs; the horrible, rubbishy mash of carparks and shopping centres and fast-food restaurants and home improvement superstores.

Sometimes, late at night in the summer heat, we walk around Oakleigh together. He lectures on and on, sailing over the footpath on his higher plane, talking about models of modern government, about astronomy, and the way computer simulations hold the key to understanding everything. I can hardly breathe, much less listen. All I can think about is the way the stone lions in the front yards look like they're frozen in mute agony, mouths grimacing, manes subdued in plaster.

'I feel like I'm dying when I come out here,' I once told him. 'Like I'm a plant whose roots are drying out in this clay-dead, chemical-dump soil.'

'Stop being so melodramatic,' he snapped.

With implacable but questionable logic, Isaac says that if I can't be happy where I am now, then I can't be happy anywhere. 'Think of it as an exercise in self-willed contentment. Accept and tolerate. *Choose* your state of mind.' He sounds like a smug Buddha as he shuffles off in his ugg boots to his thin-walled study in our beige and apricot ticky-tacky 'villa'. I give him the finger behind his back and mutter about the elimination of suffering, *my* suffering, which is obviously not part of his doctrine.

Now I've finally prised Isaac away from the green glow of his electric screen. He's here for our holiday with my dearest, oldest friends, in the city of my past. And all he can do is abuse the sunshine, complain about the heat, and look with a critical eye at the sandy suburbs and declare them soulless. I feel the dead weight of him. He's like a heavy black cloud about to rain on my parade. I wish I could summon a gale-force wind to blow him far away, back to the dark hole he loves.

But now he turns around and grins at me and reaches his hand back, wriggling his beautiful fingers to signal that he wants me to reach out and hold them, which I do, leaning awkwardly forward, trying to make up after an argument that, for him, never existed.

We're back at the house. Esther leads us inside, chattering all the while – hostess babble about where the keys are kept, how to use the air conditioner and 'help yourself to anything in the fridge'.

Isaac leaves his suitcase in the hallway and flops long-limbed into the velveteen lounge, one leg up over the arm and his head back in the cushions. 'Come here, woman.' He pulls me onto his lap. He's got his arms around me and one hand on my left breast – he's groping me, right in front of Esther, who stands on the step, looking down into the sunken room with an awkward smile. I wouldn't mind so much if Isaac's grab was really an act of lust or love or even a genuine joke, but it's the fact that he's doing it for her, as an act of possession – or an act of aggression that's supposed to warn her off me, I think – that makes me so angry and embarrassed.

I wriggle away and move into the kitchen, saying I'll get the champagne that Esther left in the freezer before we went to the airport. Unbeknown to me, she's lined the freezer door with her mother's best crystal flutes, getting them icy cold for our welcoming celebration. I'm thinking about the groping and I'm moving like an angry person, with big wide gestures, wanting to hear things bang, wanting to be loud and cross. I fling open the freezer door with all my strength. Crystal flies everywhere, the crash of disaster with a tinkling after-echo.

We're all silent for a moment. Esther's looking at me, and I'm looking at her, and Isaac comes in from the other room to see what's happened.

'What the hell have you done?' he says.

'I'm so sorry,' I cry, reaching out to Esther.

'It's nothing, honestly,' she says, picking her way across the floor to get a dustpan and broom.

But it's not nothing. It's an omen. It's fifty years of bad luck, or one week of it at least, and we all feel the shiver of a curse upon our holiday.

A few minutes later, when the mess is cleaned up and new glasses are found, the fizz is poured. Clink, clink. We say, 'Cheers!' and tilt our throats back for the awkward champagne suck. But there's a ripple of fear in the bubbles. How can things recover after such a start?

~ℒ

When we've finished our drinks I take Isaac up into the bedroom to unpack. He looks down at the bed.

'Are the sheets clean?' he asks, imperious. 'I don't want to sleep in the same sheets as Jay.'

'They're very clean,' I say bitterly. 'They're very clean, and so am I.'

He gazes at me, his great golden eyes mournful. 'Sorry,' he says, and reaches out, pulling me in close and wrapping his arms around me. I can smell the sweet aftershave I bought him for our first wedding anniversary. Just a few squirts left in the bottle now. But the base notes I sniff on his shirt are eucalyptus, from the laundry detergent we use. He smells like home and I don't want to be home. I'm still on holiday.

'I'm sorry, it's just that I've missed you,' he says into my hair. 'And knowing you were here with Jay was harder than I thought it was going to be.'

I put my lips to his, holding the kiss for a moment and then pulling back, so I can look at him and ask a question. 'When I'm in Melbourne, and you know that I'm off with Jay, then it's not so hard, is it?' I'm actually curious. These days it's so rare for Isaac to tell me anything real about the way he feels, especially about Jay, that I want to seize the moment.

'It's not the fucking that bothers me. I've told you that before.' He looks at me with a stern raise of his beautiful eyebrows. They're drawn like careful black parentheses onto his paleness. 'In Melbourne, you come home to me at night and you're there every morning. But this was too much. You were too far away.'

Now I want to change the subject. I don't want to be told off. I don't want the rules of the marriage to be refined and clarified so that I can't have any more holidays with Jay. I'm already planning the next trip away, this time to Adelaide. Jay wants to drive there, a whole weekend with me, to celebrate his birthday in February.

'What about you?' I ask briskly, without thinking. 'Any adventures of the fucking kind?'

He looks at me, appalled. 'As if I would have, without asking you first.'

'It would have been okay, under the circumstances,' I say, unzipping his suitcase and moving into the walk-in wardrobe to hang up his shirts. I don't want him to see my face.

'It would *not* be okay.'

I wonder if some part of him might sense that I don't know the rules anymore, and don't want to know them; that the idea of rules has come to seem like a return to religious dogma. A structure of belief that makes him feel safe and me feel trapped.

'I haven't had the heart for fucking, anyway,' he continues when I come back into the room. 'But maybe now ...' He starts kissing me, with a tongue that invades my mouth like an uninvited guest.

I feel sad for him and I want to make him feel better. But I'm also angry at his passivity, the great lumpish immovability of him. His inertia. His inability to just say: 'Stop seeing Jay.' Yes, I'd scream and kick with resistance. (Could I even give Jay up now? I doubt it.) But I would hear it loud and clear, and I would know that Isaac really wants me, really wants the marriage, more than he wants the rules and the comfort. I'd know then that he was ready to move, both physically and emotionally.

All I see now is avoidance as he kisses me hard. There's no joy in it, no gift, not even real desire, just need and anger and resentment, as he starts to undress me. I'm lifeless as a statue while he roughly runs his hands all over me, stuffs my breast into his mouth as if it's a soft bread roll, and pushes me down on the bed with his knee. Then he's putting his cock inside me even though I'm not ready for it. It hurts, it hurts! He's tearing me open in a big dry drive, and I'm digging my fingernails into his backside as hard as I can, but not pushing him away. I won't cry out because, for all my anger, I don't deserve his tenderness. My secrets rise up before my eyes – the three other men who've been inside me. The least I can do is accept this graze of pain.

Now he's burying himself into me as if he wishes he could become me, or disappear inside my body, or kill me trying to stretch my skin around his frame. I sigh at the complexity while he thrusts away. I feel dizzy and ashamed and *so* tired. I can't solve the puzzle of Isaac and me, even though I promised in my wedding vows to do so. The weight of it has almost sunk me. I've grasped at the buoy of an open marriage to save us, but I'm drifting away now, even from that.

I feel his soft hair all over my face and it smells like green apples. I feel the waxy smooth flesh of his high round arse in my hands, and he's whispering into my ear, 'I love you. God, I love you.' I think back to the first times, when each day was just another adventure to find a place and time alone where we could be naked. I remember the very first time, the way he took me with a vow and I gave him mine, and we pledged to be married as soon as we could, to make this wedding of the flesh into something the world would recognise. And now the world's holding me to it.

As memory and habit stir my body and heart, I'm feeling juicy and starting to rise up to meet him, pushing the shrouds of the sheet off us with my feet. 'I love you, I love you too,' I say. And then I'm coming in waves of familiar pleasure, with my legs wrapped around him so that he can't move away to thrust again. He's resisting and I'm holding him there, feeling like a tyrant, until I've finished with the close vibrating grind, almost motionless, that I need to climax. Then he lets himself go too, and I feel that we're coming together, a great long flash of perfect brightness.

He rolls off me and lies with his eyes shut, breathing loudly at first. I rest, singular and self-contained on my side, looking at him, feeling semen trickling its way out of me, down my thigh and onto the sheets. Without glancing at me, Isaac hands me a bouquet of roughly scrunched pink tissues from the bedside table. 'The chivalrous habit of a true prince,' I say with a smile, and he opens his eyes and smiles back. He's the only man I allow to flow freely inside me. What a good wife I am, I think bitterly. So careful and hygienic.

~

There's an hour or two to kill before dinner, so Isaac and I do what we do best together. We take to the bed and make it our life raft away from the sinking ship of the world outside. We grab our books and pile up the pillows, and lie side by side, with just our feet touching; we're two escapees off and away into the safe calm water of other people's written words, where we can be alone but companionable.

I watch the way his mouth moves when he's reading a choice phrase as if digesting it for future use, which he probably is. And I love the way his hair falls into his eyes and makes him look half-blind, like a wandering sage. I love the idea of that great sick brain of his, with its photographic memory, and all those numbers and words and musical notes clicking over in patterns of complex beauty. I love the idea of that brain at work, right there beside me, as if I might absorb some of its brilliance. He calls me an intellectual groupie, and I know this is true. He says in my own way I'm smarter than him, which I don't believe; I'm not smart enough to work him out.

I turn back to my own book – Hemingway's last, unfinished novel, *The Garden of Eden* – and marvel at the way his macho terseness unfolds a marriage, unwraps the love and magic and entwined co-dependency of the central couple, revealing its sickness and danger. A doomed marriage. It's too close to home so I throw it away, sliding down under the cool sheet, feeling safe and afraid all at once. Yet sleep comes quickly.

It took Isaac and me a full year to learn how to sleep together, to sail into the calm depths of synchronised breath and synchronised turning; for me to learn to sleep a little colder and for him to learn to sleep a little hotter, with his long bony feet seeking relief outside the heavy feather quilt we received as a wedding present. Four years later, it's as if we were born sleeping together. As if we once shared the same womb. As if we were, after everything, really one flesh. My brother, my husband, my Adam, our ribs moulded by the same hand.

From the shallow consciousness of early sleep I feel him nuzzle into my neck and kiss it gently before he moves away, his breath slowing. And I fall into the deepest rest I've had in weeks.

~♡

Esther and Claudia are making a special dinner to welcome Isaac, and when we come downstairs the kitchen is full of noise and light and the smell of fresh coriander being bruised on the chopping board. Claudia, who's just got home from work at the bank, rushes over and kisses Isaac on the cheek. He grabs her and twirls her around, ballroom style, into the lounge room. I watch from the doorway.

'How are you, you gorgeous creature? Look at you!' he says, admiring her form-fitting black office wear and making the sign of a curvy figure eight with his hands.

'No, look at *you*!' she shrieks. 'Gosh, you're white, even whiter than me! Are you alright?'

'Just fine and dandy. You're too used to seeing sun-damaged skin here in the Wild West.'

'You're not going to let Eve make you sunbake, are you? She's been at the beach non-stop and she's going to regret it when the wrinkles come in.'

'She does love her sun,' says Isaac simply, looking over at me, and I hear a double-meaning.

'I don't get enough at home,' I call out mischievously. 'I need to get as much as I can while I'm on holiday.'

'Bitch!' he yells, but there's no malice in it.

Now they're laughing and talking and flicking through old records, looking for The Beatles and ABBA and other relics they can sing to. I lean on the bench and smile at Esther, who's watching the pair of them. Is she envious? Claudia is simple and sweet to Isaac. She's the kind of friend who's never made demands of me, never staked her territory or made claims on the longevity of our connection. Where Esther and I will count down the years of our sisterhood, celebrating each one as a magical milestone – sometimes to taunt Isaac, who can never rival our numbers – Claudia will just smile and look surprised when I remind her that she and I share primary school photos.

Isaac also loves Claudia because she once deigned to sleep with him, when Esther never would.

'Doesn't it feel strange?' whispers Esther, pouring me a glass of wine. 'Knowing that they've been in your bed together? That he fucked her with you in the next room?'

'It feels like a relief, actually,' I say, and I mean it. 'Finally one of my friends wanted to sleep with him after him giving me free rein with his.' I think back to conflicts I've had with Isaac, problems in the open marriage, because it's so easy for me to find men who want me and so hard for him to find women who can accept our arrangement – and of course this has just compounded his original problem of feeling undesired by all the women in the world who aren't me.

Esther still seems disbelieving. 'Weren't you jealous at all, of Claudia?'

'Honestly, no,' I say, remembering the winter a year ago when Claudia visited. 'I felt motherly and generous, like giving your two kids a treat and hearing them enjoy it.'

'Yuck,' says Esther. 'That's so off.' But she giggles and moves in closer with her blue eyes wide and curious, pushing me to tell it all over again, as if new juice might erupt if she squeezes a little harder. She's so interested and without judgement, and that's why it's possible to tell her everything: about the candles and the red wine and the hangovers the next morning, and the way it went on for a couple of days. Then it was time for Claudia to catch the plane home and it never happened again.

'I was relieved myself when I first heard about it,' says Esther. 'Claudia hadn't had sex for a year, and when she came home she was happy and glowy. She even started wearing clothes that showed her boobs again.' Claudia has a tendency to dress like a Laura Ashley spinster when she hasn't had a man for a while, and she's often without a man.

'You'd think she'd get more slutty and sexy the longer she'd been without sex,' I say, pondering it and thinking of the way I am. 'But the urge just seems to dry up for her.'

'D'you think she even wanks?' says Esther.

'She must. Everybody does.'

'Some people really don't.' Esther's eyes are wide over the rim of her glass.

'I can't believe that.' I don't want to believe there are pure souls who exist in a realm so different from mine that I wonder if we're really of the same species. What must they do with their fingers at night before sleep? How do they sleep at all? What must their love-making be like when they've never rehearsed solo, learning the dark and sticky paths to their own pleasure? Can they ever find their way?

Esther's ripping apart the white flabby body of a plucked chicken, tearing away the drumsticks and shoving her hand up into the cavity so that two fingers wave out the top of the neck. I scream in genuine horror at the goose-pimpled hand-puppet. To be raised a vegetarian is to be forever aware of the deadness of meat. Even though I eat it, love it and crave it, I can never quite shake the conviction that meat is the evidence of a world fallen from grace, where the lion cannot lie down with the lamb.

But Esther has no such qualms. Her Adventist mother could never keep the meat away from a family of non-believing carnivores, and so Esther lived with the duality of spinach pie on Saturday and barbecued sausages and steak on Sunday; of sparkling grape juice sitting in the fridge next to a six-pack of beers. Whenever I opened that fridge on my many visits and sleepovers, it suggested to me a marriage with so much love

175

in it, and so much persistence, that it could withstand such clashing contradictions. It was an inspiration, though I vowed never to be so unequally yoked with an unbeliever, as Paul the Apostle had advised in his letter to the Corinthians.

Isaac comes into the kitchen in time to see Esther marinating the chicken pieces in chilli, coriander and soy sauce. 'Ooh, goody!' he says. '*Flesh* of the fowl for dinner!' He gives a booming Dracula laugh as he swipes a handful of nuts from the bowl and shoves them in his big mouth, spilling a few on the floor.

Esther hands him the cheese grater and a knob of ginger, asking him to grate it and mash it into the marinade. He flaps around, big and awkward and lazy, an expert in the art of learnt helplessness. With a frustrated sigh, she shoves him out of the kitchen, wadding a cold can of beer into his hand. 'You're useless!' she says, and it's a joke, but Isaac turns back, good humour draining from his face. He gives Esther a look that should turn her to ice, but she ignores him. I grab his arm and tell him to come out into the garden and get some air.

His skin is so thin I can see through it. Esther's joking jabs will pierce him over and over, I realise, until he's leaking on our fun and making a mess of the holiday. I'll be rushing to staunch the flow like a desperate madwoman on a sinking ship, stuffing the holes with rags of reassurance.

Out in the garden I take his hand and lead him up to the back fence where the peppermint tree is spilling over. I part the draped curtains of its streamer boughs and we're inside, in the semi-dark, with the dirt beneath our bare feet where the grass won't grow. The smell is divine and I bite down on a fresh leaf, savouring the bitter juice. 'Try it,' I say, and he does, but he wrinkles his nose. I tell him about the times Esther and I used to sit here as little girls, chewing on the leaves and playing with our dolls. I think I'm sharing it with him, but the story just makes him cross.

'You're like a club of two and you exclude me,' he says.

'You exclude yourself.'

'Be honest. You wish I wasn't here. Then the two of you could sit around reminiscing and stroking each other's hair. But then it wouldn't be any fun, would it? I mean, private jokes are only fun when you've got outsiders who don't get them.'

'You're being paranoid.'

'No, I'm not. Claudia feels it too. You can see it. She's too sweet to make a fuss, but I don't know how she stands to be around the two of you sometimes.'

'We love Claudia!'

'She's a witness to your gang of two, isn't she? You let her in and shut her out as it suits you. The handmaiden to your magic bond.'

'Stop being such a jealous pig.'

'Stop being such a selfish bitch.'

I'm so angry I could hit him. His logic and insight, twisted as they are by insecurity, haven't completely abandoned him. I feel for him; I know there's some truth in his point of view.

And so, as I've learnt to do in the last four years, I squash down my indignation, shut my eyes and take a deep breath. I stand in front of him, taking his hands in mine, and when I look up at him, I force the gentleness to come into my eyes and my voice.

'Darling,' I say, 'Esther's my best friend. My family. I see her once a year. Can't you be kind?'

'Can't *you* be kind? Aren't I your family now? Can't you start by putting me first?'

'Why does there have to be a first? Why can't we all be together?'

'Because I'm your husband, and I have to come first.'

I bow my head and want to scream, because I hear the Old Testament in his voice. Crude stone tablets are being brought in to settle a subtle dispute – overkill. In his tone is the authority that tells me woman must be subordinate to man, and that man is the head of the household, as it is in Isaac's family and in mine. Even though Isaac pretends to be modern – going so far as to let me share my body with other men – in his heart he's archaic. He's wistfully patriarchal.

Of course he won't admit it; he thinks he's a feminist. But I don't have the energy to argue with the phantoms of his sexism right now. I feel like shouting into his hurt face that yes, I do wish he'd never come on this holiday. Yes, it's easier without him. And no, he doesn't come first in everything.

Instead I kiss his hands, remembering the promises I've made to him. So many of them broken, not least of all the quixotic pledge to tell him the truth in everything. Can the centre hold when that promise has been shattered? But I won't abandon him. Not tonight – and, I tell myself, not ever.

'I'll try harder,' I say. 'I really will. And I'm glad you're here, darling.'

He looks at me hopefully and tries to smile off the fight.

~⚬

The dinner table has been laid out as if it's the set of a play, with silver, crystal, candles and the best china. Mozart's on the record player – Isaac's choice. We eat our chicken and drink our wine, and laugh out loud at Claudia's tales of bureaucratic stupidity at the tax office and difficult customers at the nightclub. She's a gifted mimic of voices, and I wonder at the intelligence of her perceptions – the fact that she truly sees these things, even if she could never write them down the way I could.

I love Claudia's intricate bitchy accounts of the households where she cleans in her other part-time job. Those pampered Claremont bitches, doctors' and lawyers' wives, manage to avoid being alone with their children for more than an hour or two, even though they don't work. It breaks Claudia's heart because she loves children and wants a brood of her own, once she has the husband and the big house with polished floorboards to accommodate them. She'll be a different kind of rich lady: a loving mother who cleans her own toilet.

After dinner, Isaac picks up the old guitar in the corner and brushes off the dust. He tunes the strings and begins to play softly, and we soon stop talking because he's so good. He's hunched over the instrument with his hair covering his face. His lovely white fingers, so strong and sure, are all I can see, and I long for them to touch me with that assurance, that concentration.

I remember him playing his sea-green jewel of an electric guitar in his bedroom, back when we were all shy and new. His forearm tensed and flexed as he strummed, enough to make me impatient with desire to fuck him. Weeks later, when he'd played at a weekend camp for Adventist university students, he was the only one lighting up the stage: a loud and outrageously camp version of The Troggs' 'Wild Thing', as he looked straight at me and snarled the lyrics. We fucked in a single bed that night, and slept, or mostly didn't sleep, clinging to each other as if on a precipice, hoping that no dorm counsellor would catch us and send us home with a lecture on premarital sex.

Now Isaac's playing ancient tunes I love, like the mournful 'Greensleeves', his lovely voice unmarked by any irony or self-consciousness. I love him. I pity him. I can't live without him. He's my injured creature and I am his. He looks up and winks at me; I feel tied to him forever and I'm glad.

~

In the morning, he wakes up with a fever. His face is so hot I can hardly bear to touch it, and the sheets are tangled and wet with sweat. I can't believe I've slept so soundly while he's been awake, tortured with nausea all night. He says there's nothing left in his stomach.

'Why didn't you wake me?' I say.

'You looked so peaceful,' he moans.

'Can I get you anything?'

'A glass of water would be good … with a little squeeze of lemon and ginger?'

'Sure.'

'And would you mind bringing me a cold flannel and a bowl of ice?'

'Okay.'

'And could you turn the fan up?'

'Yep.'

This is the limit of my desire to nurse him – I've reached it already, in less than five minutes. I look at his white face and his sweaty hair, and I want to run away. I'm cross that he's sick on the first real day of our holiday together. Did he do it on purpose? Is it some kind of trick to make me his slave and keep me inside this dark bedroom? To harness my full attention?

He sees the pained look on my face. 'You haven't got an ounce of compassion, have you?'

'I do! I want to make you feel better. But you know how I am with sick people – it's irrational. I *do* care, but I feel like I'm going to stop breathing when I have to look after someone.'

'It's pathetic.'

'I know, I know,' I agree. 'It's a fucked-up survival trait, to leave the sick for dead and escape. I'm evolving – can't you see? – because at least I can acknowledge it.' I'm trying for a joke, but he's not buying it. His mother, his ex-girlfriend and his sister are all nurses, professional ones with university degrees, but also with natural softness and cool, comforting hands. I know I'm a disappointment to him; he should have married someone like that.

'You're a monster,' he tells me. 'Get me some water and then leave me to *die* here alone.' The melodramatic way he says this softens it a little, and we both force a smile. But we're angry with old anger from old fights.

I get the water and the ice and then leave, slamming the door. Glad to be told to get out, but hating myself. I *am* heartless – he's right. But this is only half the story.

I won't stop worrying about him, or suffering with him, through visits to the doctor, through fortunes spent at the chemist, and through stinking hot nights of him tossing and turning and vomiting beside me. This is a kind of hell and I suspect I deserve it. I am the witch with the poisoned apple. I am his bad fruit, and there's no cure for me.

Over the next few days, my escape from the sick room is the telephone downstairs. My calls to Jay light up the early evenings, as the sun starts to set and dinner is being made.

'Isaac's still sick. Another ghastly day.' I sigh.

'Poor baby. And by that I mean *you*!' I hear the gurgle in his laugh.

'Isaac's so white. So pale. Actually, he's beautifully tubercular.' I think of my husband leaning wanly against the snowy pillows, and remember the rush of love that filters through my annoyance as I bring him more Panadol or more cold flannels.

'Beautifully tubercular,' repeats Jay. 'I'm going to keep that for future reference.'

'Yeah, he's like a dying eighteenth-century poet, only more annoying.'

'Well, at least he's not faking it. That would be intolerable.'

'He's not faking it,' I say. 'I really have been worried about him. But I can't help wondering if he subconsciously willed it. To punish me.'

'Silly girl! Stop giving in to the guilt,' says Jay. 'You're reading too much into it.'

Jay doesn't like to talk about my guilt. He elides it, letting it slide off him and into some other realm. Being around him makes it easier for me to forgive myself, but it's a shallow and fleeting forgiveness. I always need more of him to make me feel better. I can feel the addiction growing.

'What about you?' I ask. 'What's happening there?'

'Long, long days. Counting the hours till I see you again. Trying to distract myself. Last night I saw Angelique. We got dinner at the Galleon and walked down to the St Kilda pier.'

'Nice. Is she still living with the drug dealer?'

I know a great deal about Angelique, though I've never met her. I know the length of her hair, the shape of her arse ('like a pear, hung low, but peachy'), what she looks like lying naked on a bed. There are photos of her in Jay's albums, and he remembers his time with her fondly.

'Yeah, she's still with him. She likes getting it for free. It's been six months since we –'

'Yeah, right, whatever.' I don't want him going down memory lane right now. 'Does she flirt with you?' I'm curious, but also concerned. I have no right to be jealous … but I am, a bit.

'We talked about you the whole time,' he says, 'though at one point she did fuck my thumb.'

'*What?*' I feel my armour snapping into place, ready to protect me. I imagine his thumb, his knobby fingers and smooth hands, not roughed by work, sliding up Angelique's skirt as she pushes her wet druggy cunt down hard on his thumb. Where did it happen? While they were sitting on his lounge-room floor chatting after dinner? At the beach late at night?

'No, you misheard! She *sucked* my thumb,' he says, laughing. 'We were eating ice-cream.'

'Oh. That's alright then.'

'It better be. You're in bed every night with another man, remember. Albeit a half-dead one.'

'I wish I was in your bed. Right now.'

'I wish you were too,' Jay says. 'I don't know how I'm going to get through the next ten days.'

'Me either.'

~⌒

Finally, on Christmas Eve, the worst of the sickness has passed and Isaac is able, wanly, and still looking beautifully pale, to join the three of us in celebration. While he's been away in his darkened room, we've been dressing the tall fake tree with all the costume jewellery in the house, big plastic pearls and glass diamonds, mixed up with strings of fresh white popcorn, red silk flowers and tiny Victorian-style painted wooden toys that we found at the Reject Shop. Like happy orphans, Esther and I are loving the fact that for the first time ever, we have no parents to worry about this Christmas. For Claudia, who really is an orphan, it's no novelty, and she'll spend the day with her grandmother and her brother, remembering the parents she lost.

But this Christmas Eve is ours, and we're trying for English tradition despite the heat. Esther has made a plum pudding (laboriously, and with many long-distance phone calls to her mother in Hong Kong), and I have deigned to stuff my hand up a turkey's bum and fill it with a fragrant mix of fresh herbs and breadcrumbs. Now Claudia is making the brandy butter to go with the pudding, beating the creamy mixture and splashing in the liquor with a liberal hand, stopping often to swipe her finger through and lick it clean. We have Frank Sinatra and Bing Crosby on the record player, and Isaac sings along as if this qualifies as some kind of contribution.

After we've eaten, we gather around the tree for the gift-giving. Five-dollar presents is the game we've devised. The thrift is the challenge, to find something perfect or quirky or funny for that nominal fee. Despite their cheapness, the gifts are wrapped with luxurious care: thick embossed paper and iridescent satin ribbons adorned with tiny, tinkling silver bells. Isaac plays Santa while I hold the camera, recording the moments of grand opening.

For Claudia, Esther has found an op-shop treasure, a lime-green glass lemon-squeezer that will sit squat and handsome in her collection of retro-kitsch glassware. For Isaac, I've found a tie that's so hideous it's gorgeous: fake white silk, with an Asian landscape sketched across it in rough charcoal hues. He ties it round his neck on top of his t-shirt, a careful Windsor knot remembered from our church school uniforms. For me, Isaac has found a set of plastic babushka dolls, brightly and delicately painted in my favourite hues of gold and red.

When it's time for Claudia's gifts, Esther takes the first one, a mysteriously heavy box. She opens it. It's a leather-bound set of Jane Austen's works. Claudia smiles expectantly, and guiltily.

Esther stares back. She's cross. 'Five dollars?'

'But it was too hard,' says Claudia, trying to be winsome. 'And I wanted to get you something really nice. Don't you like it? You love Jane Austen.'

'I love them, but you broke the rules,' says Esther coldly.

'I'm sorry,' says Claudia, rebuked.

I try to make the peace, urging us all to move on and open the other gifts, but it doesn't get better. For Isaac it's a glossy book of black-and-white photographs of sixties London, and for me a pair of jet earrings and a matching string of shiny black beads. Esther glowers, and Claudia's upset.

The night disintegrates into the lonely tinkling of dishes being washed, garbage being taken out, and cupboards being slammed open and shut. Isaac and I sit on the couch, my legs thrown over his. We try to flip through his beautiful new book, but we're watching, almost relieved as somebody else's conflict takes precedence over our own. I realise then that even when you think you've escaped family, flown a thousand miles to spend it with friends instead, Christmas can be so fraught and disappointing. Being together can be so hard.

~

'Merry Christmas, Dad!' I'm on the phone in the bedroom upstairs, looking out the window over the yards and houses where other people will be celebrating with their families today.

'Merry Christmas, darling,' he says. 'Wish you were here.'

My parents have been in the Solomon Islands for a year, but I haven't visited them there yet. I can't quite picture their house, even though I've seen photos of the boxy Queenslander on stilts, the coconut trees out the back, and the frangipani and hibiscus in the front yard, which Mum says I'd love.

'I know, next year, I promise,' I say. 'But we wanted to be here with Esther for a change. She's an orphan this year.'

'How is Esther?' he asks fondly. He likes her, remembers the delightful child she was, a 'positive influence' on me despite her pierced ears and heathen father.

'She's good, Dad. She's been studying hard. We had fun last night, and she's having Christmas with her brothers at her auntie's house in Applecross.'

'What about you and Isaac? Where will you go?'

'We're having a quiet one. He's been crook with a virus.'

'Is he okay? Has he been to the doctor?'

'Yeah, he's fine,' I say, not wanting to go into boring details. 'We might go down to Rossmoyne for a picnic, just the two of us, by the river.'

'But aren't you going to Auntie Marg's? Nana and your cousins will be there. They'd love to have you.' His voice is so hopeful. He likes to imagine me in the bosom of his family, even though they're not important enough for him to be here himself.

'Nah. We'll give it a miss.'

Silence. He's hurt. 'Have you even rung them?'

'Soon. But maybe don't mention we're here when you speak to them. It'd be awkward.'

'It'll be awkward if they run into you on the street and find out you've been there for weeks,' he says. 'Perth's a small place, remember?'

'Don't hassle me, I will.'

'Okay, love.' He sighs. 'God bless. I'll put Mum on.'

There's shuffling in the background and muffled voices. My brother is there with two friends from the Adventist University where they're all studying to be teachers and accountants. They'll probably work for the Church when they're finished and marry the good girls they've met there. Aiden is my opposite in all things intellectual, religious and sporting. It's amazing we sprang from the same womb, our almond eyes and straight white teeth the only things we share.

The boys will go snorkelling later on, an hour up the coast where Mum and Dad have their favourite beach spot. There's a World War II shipwreck close to the shore, and the coral and fish are more plentiful and brighter than in the Barrier Reef; you only have to wade waist-deep to see it all. Well, that's what Mum's letters say when she's trying to entice me to visit.

'Hi, darling,' she says, sounding anxious. 'Isaac's not well?' She's been sitting beside Dad, trying to catch my news.

'Merry Christmas, Mum,' I say, irritated already by the way she assumes the worst; the way she can't stop worrying. 'Yeah, he's been sick, but he's on the mend now. It's been so annoying.'

Why do I always tell her more than I want to? As if the sound of her voice is truth serum.

'Poor Isaac,' she says, sympathetic. 'Are you being nice to him?'

'Yes, Mum, I'm trying. But it's a pain in the neck that he got sick on our holiday.' I know I sound like a petulant child.

'It's not his fault. Try to be loving, darling. Even if you don't feel it.'

'I know, I know,' I say impatiently. 'But it's so hard sometimes.'

'I know.'

And I know that she does understand, because she's a wife who finds it hard herself. She's always been open with me about that, even when I was a little girl. Back then I was her only confidante, the only one she'd share the struggle with, because to air her grievances publicly might hurt Dad's standing in the Church. I've seen her resentments played out all my life – the conflicts over where to live, how to spend money and where exactly the Holy Spirit might be leading us next. But because Mum's endured thirty years of a difficult marriage, and actually kept on loving and forgiving, I know it's possible. I know it's what I have to do.

Even if I'm doing it in my own way.

10

The week between Christmas and New Year's Eve feels flat and dead. Sleepy Perth seems even more of a ghost town than usual, the shops desultorily opening their doors only if they absolutely have to, and then with restricted hours. The sales staff are grumpy because they haven't slept well in the night-time heat. Those who are lucky enough have migrated 'down south' to Dunsborough and Busselton and Margaret River, the cooler climes of wine, cheese and surf country. Esther has suggested we try to find somewhere to stay down there, make the trip to show Isaac the places we spent our school holidays – the Margaret River mouth, where we'd lie on the rocks where the river met the ocean, feeling the warm brackish water mingling with the fresh cold waves; the bush where we'd camp and grow dirty and brown, our hair smelling of eucalyptus and smoke. But Isaac's not keen on this idea, and none of us has any money for accommodation.

Isaac's not keen on many of our ideas, including the beach; he shudders at the mention of it.

'Let's have a picnic in Kings Park, then,' says Esther one

bright blue day when Claudia is off work. Isaac agrees, so the four of us pack the car and make the drive, the Swan River sparkling and laughing on our left as we pass South Perth and Como and head across the bridge. Then we're up, up through West Perth and out into the world's most beautiful park, an oasis of iridescent green in a city that's always brown and parched in summer.

I love this place, one of the rare spots where you can look out over the city and the river, with the futuristic swirl of fast-flowing freeways circling across and around it. We drive through the avenue of stately ghost gums, each commemorating a fallen soldier, and past the war memorial and its wall of engraved names where as children we'd whisper sacrilegiously stupid messages, waiting for the echo to travel around the curve.

We're headed into the heart of the park now, where there's bush and green lawns on all sides, a botanical garden with no view of the city.

'The Pioneer Lady!' I cry as I see her, that nine-foot-tall bronze statue, a sturdy but graceful woman holding her baby on her hip and balancing on a stepping stone in the greeny-brown pond. Bubbling fountains spurt up around her in a three-minute sequence, small squirts building to large ones that represent the bushland to be cleared, way back then. There's nothing wild about this sheltered place, with shady trees on one slope and gazebos and picnic tables on the other.

'What's the day today?' asks Esther. 'Oh my god, it's Sabbath. I hope it won't be swarming with Sevs!'

'So why are we coming to the Pioneer Lady if you don't want to bump into them?' asks Claudia.

This is where the Adventists would picnic on warm Sabbath afternoons, congregating in family groups around the fountain. My dad, a minor celebrity with a patient ear, was always in demand. Long into the afternoon, Mum, Aiden and I would be waiting for him to finish his work, which involved a lot of nodding and smiling and discussing the theological intricacies of the Book of Revelation.

The best times were when Mum let me bring Esther back from church with us, and she and I would meander off on our own, removing our high heels and dipping our hot swollen feet into the pond, giggling about who'd kissed who at Fellowship the night before. Sometimes Marcus and his family would be gathered on the opposite side of the pond – their traditional spot – and he and I would go for slow wanders deep into the hot cicada-busy bush, where we'd sweat and kiss in the blazing sun, him in his long pants, shirt and tie, and me in my tailored skirt suit and stockings.

'It's our place as much as theirs,' says Esther defiantly as she parks the car. 'Actually, I hope they do see us. While we're smoking and drinking wine.'

'Rebel,' says Isaac indulgently.

'Well, I hope they don't see us,' says Claudia. 'It would kill Granny if she heard about it.'

'And I hope my relatives aren't here.' I suddenly think of the awfulness if my nana and cousins happen to be picnicking after church. 'Surprise, I'm here in Perth, and I just didn't want to see you!' I say, imagining it.

But as we lug our rugs and baskets down the slope to the shade on the right of the pond, there are no Sevs in sight. The fountain spits peacefully as the Pioneer Lady stares across the empty manicured lawn. A cool breeze blows. I'm almost disappointed that it's deserted.

After we've eaten our cold chicken and potato salad, and spread the fast-warming blue cheese on crackers, and drunk white wine (out of real glasses because Esther refuses to drink from plastic), we're lying on the rugs, bellies full, and looking up through the branches into the clear blue sky. Perfect white clouds, small and unthreatening, scud past with the breeze, and I woozily watch dragons turn into bears and then into cats and castles and trains with steam trailing behind them.

'The clouds are so beautiful,' I say slowly, my arms spread wide, fingers reaching out across the rough grass that's tickling my wrist.

'You're drunk, my love,' says Isaac, and leans over to kiss me. I grab his head and hold him there longer than he'd intended. I like the feel of him, the smell of him and the way a strand of his long dark hair brushes my cheek. He lets me kiss him, but I can tell he wants to pull away.

'Always such a loving drunk, though,' says Esther affectionately, watching us and pouring herself more wine. 'I always know when I see a photo of you, Eve, how much you've had to drink by how tightly you've got your arms wrapped around someone. Or your face pushed up close to them.'

'Hey, I'm not that drunk!' I protest. 'I just love the world. And you.'

'Of course you do, darling.' She lies next to me so that the crook of my arm is under her head. I can feel her hot gold hair and the sweat of her neck. 'See that cloud up there,' she says, 'the one that's all runny and oozy and separating?'

'Yes!' I look eagerly for the pattern she might be seeing in it.

'Looks just like our blue cheese.'

'Don't tease me.' I move my cool feet so they're in the dappled sunshine while the rest of me is in the shade.

~~◦~~

After a while, Claudia's getting restless and Isaac says he's bored. He wants to climb to the top of the famous DNA Tower, with its double-helix staircases, on the hill behind us.

'Are you sure?' I ask, thinking of the two hundred steps and the fact Isaac's not completely well yet. He's usually so sedentary that the idea of him voluntarily expending energy seems odd.

'I do, actually,' he says. 'I've heard you can see Rottnest Island from the top. And I just love the idea of a staircase in the shape of DNA.'

'Of course you do, *nerd*,' I say with a laugh.

'Come on,' says Claudia, standing up and offering her hand to pull him off the grass. 'I'll take you. Just don't faint on me in your delicate state, okay? I can't carry you down.'

'Thank you, my dear,' he says, courtly.

And the two of them are away, leaving Esther and me lolling tipsily in the late afternoon light. I can hear birds and the sound of traffic in the distance. A child yells out, 'Found you!' in a far-off game of hide-and-seek. A fly buzzes near my ear. I can almost hear the grass growing.

'Hey,' Esther says, turning to me, eyes bright with an idea, 'let's try a game I played last week.'

'I hate games,' I say flatly, and it's true. Scrabble, Monopoly, softball, cards – I lose interest so quickly. What's the point of winning, anyway? I hate to compete. Or maybe I just hate to lose.

'No, you'll like this game. It's a bit psychological.' Esther lies back and adjusts her straw hat so it covers half her face. All I can see are her pink lips and the tip of the perfect little nose that reminds me of a rabbit's when she wrinkles it. 'There are no right or wrong answers,' she explains. 'Just shut your eyes and tell me the first picture that comes into your mind when I ask the questions.'

'Okay,' I say, closing my eyes and giving in to her voice.

'Alright. You're in a forest. Describe it to me.'

'It's a glade of pine trees. Pretty. The sun's coming in. I'm walking along a path.'

'There's an object in front of you – what is it?' she asks.

'It's sparkly. It's pretty. Like a brooch, a little piece of junk jewellery. Or maybe it's just a shiny lolly wrapper.' I picture the object twinkling there in front of me on the ground.

'And what do you do with it?'

'I pick it up, put it in my pocket. But I know it's rubbish. A bit tacky, really.'

'Now there's some water in front of you. What's it like?'

'It's a waterfall. Gushing and rushing. There are rapids. It's loud, overwhelming.'

'Really?' She laughs, and I wonder what this can mean. 'How do you get to the other side?'

'I don't know! It's too dangerous.'

'So what do you do?'

'I guess I'll have to jump in and swim, but I might get carried away.'

'Let's just say you get to the other side somehow,' she says, moving me along from my dismay. 'You walk for a while and see a barrier you need to get over. What's it like?'

'A brick wall, high and grey, and I'm going to have to climb it with my toes and fingers. I'll have to find crevices and pull myself up. But it's going to hurt.'

'Let's say you've climbed it. What's on the other side?'

I think hard and long. It all seems blank at first. Blackness. Nothing. But then it rises up before me, sparkling and white like an ivory palace. 'It's a shopping centre,' I say. 'A big, beautiful shopping centre, glass and marble, full of things I'd love to buy.' I pause, moving closer to the image. 'But it's shut. The lights are off. I've come at the wrong time and I can't get in.'

'Oh, Eve.' She sits up with her hat off and her eyes open. 'Darling, that's funny and sad.'

'Why, what does it mean?' I'm worried now.

'It's just a stupid game. Don't worry.'

'I *am* worried now!'

Esther sighs. 'Okay, here's what it's all supposed to symbolise. The forest is your life and the way you see it. You like it. The sun's shining in and the trees are pretty. They say that people who see a path or a road in front of them are still searching for their purpose. Which I guess you are.'

'I am,' I admit. 'I'm a bit lost. But it's okay.'

'Yes, it's okay. And the object on your path is your attitude to material things.'

'My tacky brooch?'

'Yes. I don't think you're gonna be rich, because you don't want it enough!' She pauses, picking at a weed and pulling it out – she just can't help herself. 'But you did put it in your pocket. That's something.'

'Okay. And what about the water?'

'Oh dear. It's sex!' She laughs. 'Desire and sex and love. I think you've got too much going on there. You feel like you're drowning and you don't know how to get to the other side.'

'How embarrassing. If I'd known, I would have conjured myself up a bridge!'

'It doesn't work like that,' she says. 'No, this is all good stuff, the keys to your unconscious.'

'But what about you?' I ask, curious. 'What was your answer?'

'A babbling brook, fast flowing but with stepping stones across it.' She smiles and sticks her tongue out at me. I wonder at the ease with which things come to her, the way life seems to shine on her and light a path simpler than mine.

'And the fence or the wall, what does that mean?' I ask.

'It's how you see death. It's an obstacle to you. High and daunting, but you face up to it, even though you know it's going to hurt.'

'And the thing on the other side then ... is Heaven?' I feel myself go cold at the idea, even though I'm right in the sun now.

'It's your vision of the afterlife,' she says gently. 'You think it's a place filled with good things. But you don't have the keys and it's shut off from you now.'

'Oh! That's a little bit tragic.'

'What's a little bit tragic?' asks Isaac, flopping onto the blanket, puffed out from his walk up the staircase to nowhere. Claudia sinks down beside him.

'Eve doesn't believe in God anymore, but still believes in Heaven *and* that she's not going to be allowed in,' says Esther

– a little blithely, I think, given we've just unravelled my spiritual tragedy.

'Maybe she does still believe in God, deep down?' says Claudia, munching on a bunch of cold green grapes she's dug out of the esky.

'There is no God,' I say, feeling the familiar thrill of speaking it aloud. (But I still say the name with a capital letter.)

'Of course she believes in God,' says Isaac, looking at me with a superior smile. 'Why else would she be working so hard to defy him?'

I see then that Isaac does believe. And he wishes I did too.

II

It's New Year's Eve and the sun is just setting. All over the city people are waiting for it to be dark, waiting for these early evening hours to be over so they can begin the celebrations for real, begin the drinking and the kissing and the happily superstitious carnival of calendar turnover.

Esther and I are sitting out on the porch, sweating in the forty-degree heat and fanning ourselves with pages torn from *Marie Claire*. We're slapping away mosquitoes and sipping tall, icy gin and tonics. To me it tastes like the bitter chewed-up pips of lemons, but I force it down because Esther's made it for me without even asking if I wanted it.

She's been on the phone and in the car all afternoon, arranging the drugs and planning the night's progression, which she promises will be 'just so beautiful'. 'You'll look in the mirror and know you're gorgeous.' She strokes my hair. 'You'll be in love with yourself and all the beautiful people around you.'

I'm an innocent with drugs, and I hang on her every word as if she's my guide to a different planet. Her enthusiasm seems to be vibrating out of her flushed skin and the strands of blonde hair that frizz from her messy ponytail. She's radiating light in anticipation of fresh drugs. Ecstasy and speed. Love and energy.

Esther and I haven't been together on New Year's Eve for almost a decade, and this feels like we're planning a wedding of sorts: a midnight feast to remind us of the ones we had as fourteen-year-olds, replete with dramatic resolutions ('I will become braver! I *will* lose ten kilos!'), stolen wine, and sneaking out of bed to do nothing more rebellious than wait for shooting stars to wish upon.

Esther's leaning forward, holding my hand and looking into my eyes as if she's puzzling out the secrets of the universe. But really she's just asking me what she should wear tonight.

This is how Isaac finds us as he comes outside looking for me. He's been in bed all afternoon, sleeping and reading. He blinks in the light and stretches dramatically, a rumpled professor.

'What are you two cooking up?' he asks.

'Just planning the night,' says Esther.

'She's telling me about the speed and the ecstasy,' I explain, handing him my glass so he can share my drink.

Isaac scowls. 'You don't know where that stuff comes from,' he says. 'I don't think I'll be joining you on that little trip, Esther.'

Pompous git, I think.

'But we've already paid for it,' says Esther, pouting as winningly as she can. 'We've got yours here, with all the others.' She holds up the tiny packets that she's been putting in and out of her pocket since she came home an hour ago.

'Yeah, well, I think I've changed my mind,' he says as he looks meaningfully at me, 'and I think Eve should change her mind too.'

I stare back at him and say nothing. We talked about doing this, back in Melbourne. Made plans for it. Now he's turned all adult on me, giving me the anti-drugs lecture – the man who's been my playmate all these years. The man who's spent months turning our living room into his bong chamber and filling our wheelie bin with the depressive clunk of his Scotch bottles. But alcohol is safe and legal. And weed is benign – he's always telling me so, even as I push it away because I don't know how to smoke it and I don't like to. Even when he puts it into cookies for me, all I feel is a licence to binge on bad food.

'Darling,' I say, 'you're always talking about pushing back the gates of perception –'

'Yeah, but I like to know what I'm doing. I like to control it.'

'Isn't being out of control part of the point?' I ask.

'I don't like to take unnecessary risks.'

Esther and I start giggling because he sounds like a straight little swat who's just signed his Temperance Pledge, the way we all did at church when we were twelve, prompted by groups of pious, whiskery old ladies wielding pens and paper.

'Come on,' says Esther. 'Play with us, Isaac. Just for tonight. Just once. You'll be *fine*.'

But Isaac just shakes his head in disgust and goes back inside, leaving us to drink the sour brew he's made of our plans.

～◯

In Esther's bedroom we stand gazing into her mirror, which is swathed in strings of beads, silk scarves and Blu-Tacked photographs of the two of us in front of the Melbourne art gallery, and sitting on the stone purse sculpture in the Bourke Street Mall, and riding a ferry on Sydney Harbour.

We've just taken showers and we're in our G-strings. No bras tonight; our clothes won't allow it. We stand close together in front of the glass, admiring the bones that jut out on our hips, and the flat, almost concave planes of our bellies. We hold up our arms and see the narrow stretch of them, muscles elegantly defined because there's no fat left, not because we're strong. We have to push our breasts together to make any cleavage, arranging them in a semblance of voluptuousness.

'I'm losing my boobs,' I say, frowning.

'At least you've still got some,' Esther says, then, 'Hey, let's see how much we weigh!' as if it's the wickedest thing we could do together.

We run to the bathroom and stand on the scales, checking the consequences of our diets. We're pleased as we watch the old-fashioned needle struggle past seven stone for me and eight for her, because she's taller. We're fading away and we love it. But it's a temporary state, we know, and soon we'll have to eat normally again.

Back in the bedroom we get dressed. Esther's wearing tight vinyl pants of metallic silver; they shine and gleam over the sweet gentle curve of her bum. I'm wearing the matching top, a silver lace-up bodice. It stretches tight over what's left of my breasts, holds them together and pushes them up like pale puddings.

Tonight Esther and I are announcing our togetherness. We're a set. Soul twins. My top to her bottom. We paint our lips metallic pink, shade our eyes with glitter and stick on false eyelashes. We're space-age Barbarellas, weightless and giddy, innocent and sexy, visiting from a planet where gravity and morality are different.

Isaac comes in and takes a look at us. He gives a great booming laugh, walking over to kiss my neck. I guess he's gotten over his tantrum about the drugs.

'You're a pair of freakish birds,' he says with good humour. 'Gorgeous.' He pulls off a turquoise feather boa from the mirror and wraps it around himself. I can see him longing to be one of us, a bright-plumed bird himself, but he'll have to stay in boring black jeans tonight. This is Perth, after all, not the Mardi Gras or the Brunswick Street Festival, where we go with our gay friends. No lovely queens to protect him and fuss over him tonight.

He looks sad all of a sudden. I see it in his eyes, and so does Esther. She goes to him and fixes his hair. 'You look good,' she says.

'I don't feel good. In fact, I don't feel well at all. Do we have to go, Eve?'

Is he really asking me to stay at home, on New Year's Eve, after everything that's been planned? Is this some kind of test, one I can't possibly pass?

'Darling,' I say, 'you'll have fun. Let's go out for dinner and then see how you're feeling. We can always come home.'

'Can we?' he asks, wanting to be comforted and assured. 'Will Claudia be there?'

'Not for dinner, but afterwards in the city. She's working now. Then she'll come home for a nap so she can last until midnight.'

'I don't think I can last until midnight,' he says glumly.

Esther's getting impatient. She's staring into the mirror and picking at her teeth, as if to stop herself from saying something mean.

'You'll be fine. I'll look after you,' I say. But I'm no nurse. Surely he knows that by now.

~⊙~

The phone rings just before we leave the house. Jay is calling from Melbourne where he's preparing his own night out. It's been three days since I heard his voice and it makes me happy. We've been missing each other's calls; it's been hard to grab a moment with Isaac's needs and moods.

I tell Jay I'm feeling really good. 'I can't wait to have New Year's Eve with Esther and Claudia. It's been so long.'

'New Year's Eve, Eve's new year!' he says, pleased with himself. 'Have a beautiful night with your friends, darling. I just wanted to tell you that when midnight strikes here, three hours before it strikes you, I'll blow a kiss to the moon.'

'Sweet.' I sigh. 'And when it strikes here, I'll think of you too. But where should I picture you?'

He laughs. 'Probably off my face somewhere, in a hotel room on top of the city.'

'Really? With who?'

'With "whom", darling. With Alexandra and Tim, you know, my friends from Sydney. The ones who live large and take lovers. Remember? Alexandra and I had a thing back in '94 ...'

Jay launches into a story that I don't follow, full of digressions and descriptions of the way it began and the way it ended, with the gist being that they're all great friends now and they've rented a penthouse; they're going to take cocaine and ecstasy and watch fireworks from the balcony. Then they'll have baths in the spa as the sun comes up.

'I kind of wish I was there,' I say, wistfully. I'd rest my cheek on Jay's hairy wet chest.

'I'd love it too. But you enjoy tonight with your friends. And with Isaac. Is he getting better?'

'He's not totally well.' I curl the olive-green coil of wall-mounted telephone cord around my wrist to make a chunky, stretchy bracelet. 'He's kind of weird – flat and tired and annoying,' I whisper, suddenly afraid that Isaac might hear me from the next room. I'm being so disloyal.

'Poor him. Poor you. Just have fun, okay? Remember, you've been planning this night for months, so don't let anything ruin it.' He pauses, and I think of how much he wishes good things for me, wants pleasure for me. But is that because it costs him nothing? 'Better go or I'll be late,' he says, 'and Alexandra will be a bitch for the rest of the night.'

'I love you,' I say.

'I crave you,' he whispers melodramatically, and I can hear the smile in his voice.

~⊙

We have dinner in South Perth with Esther's friends who are visiting from London and renting a villa. There's a long rectangular swimming pool and a paved barbecue area, which they're using for every single meal because they think this is what Australians do.

Dinner is a too-rich meal of barbecued crabs and avocado salad. Isaac and I hardly touch it. The idea of cracking a shell and pulling apart a leggy creature in order to eat its soft belly is too much for us. We commiserate with looks across the table, trying not to laugh at the absurdity of well-dressed, civilised adults being so brutal and messy. Our forays into meat-eating still veer towards the 'clean' meats, out of habit, though with the exception of crispy bacon.

Isaac slyly sticks his tongue out the side of his mouth and makes his eyes wide at me, as if he's about to vomit. I try not to giggle while I use my paper serviette to cover the leggy blue carcass in front of me. I look at Esther, who is holding court up the other end of the table. She has a glass of champagne in one hand and a crab claw in the other, jabbing the air as she talks energetically to the old gentleman on her left. I can tell she's slipped into her English accent.

The heat is overwhelming and, after wilted pavlova and berries, I leave the table to sit on the edge of the pool. I dip my overheated, mosquito-bitten feet into the soothing blue. Isaac comes over and sits beside me, leaning against me heavily. I tell him to put his feet in, that it's lovely.

'I don't want to take my shoes off. Too much hassle.' He lies parallel to the pool on the warm concrete, resting his head in my lap and dropping his left arm into the pool, where it dangles up to the elbow, a languid, half-hearted attempt at coolness. I stroke his sweaty forehead with my wet hands, smelling of chlorine, and he shuts his eyes, humming a tune I don't recognise.

After dinner we head into the hot concrete heart of Perth, travelling past the tall office blocks, the Royal Perth Hospital and the central train station in order to get to Northbridge, that busy little square of partying madness. The bitumen pulsates with crowded heat. The digital tower says that it's 11pm and thirty-seven degrees – a rare combination, even here.

There are people everywhere, drunk and loud and waiting for something to happen. What do they expect? The men seem wild and predatory, their eyes already clouded with drink and their shirts sticky and sweaty, steaming them into restless, pink-fleshed heckling. For the first time I feel scared. Esther and I have become separated from Isaac and the English friends. A bottle smashes on the pavement ahead of us and a woman screams. Esther grabs my hand.

'Lezzos! Kiss, kiss!' comes a snarly shout from our left.

'Don't look at them,' says Esther, walking even faster than her usual lanky stride.

I scan the crowds for the comforting navy blue of police uniforms. There they are, four of them, fluorescent vests shining like beacons over their uniforms. They're a welcome sight as they take charge, talking into their radios, pointing their batons and urging the crowds to keep moving west, into the centre of Northbridge. Will we all fit?

The policemen see Esther and me. They smile as they glance at our linked hands. The taller one nudges his mate and says something out of the side of his mouth, and they laugh, just ordinary men after all, with girl-on-girl fantasies and a tendency to leer. For just a moment I wonder how much my freedom depends upon illusions of civility. Maybe I have no idea about the Real World, because I come from a place where the men are gentle and good with words; a charmed land where men play with me when I'm frisky but leave me alone when I ask them to.

Isaac eventually catches up to us and for a moment I'm relieved, grabbing his arm like a safety ring. But he pulls away and walks a little behind us, making himself alone. He's unhappy and unprotecting, obviously wondering how long he must endure the heat, the noise and my flaunted otherness. He wants me to ask him how he feels, I can tell, but I don't want to. His wan fretfulness bores and stifles me. I know I'm cruel, but I don't care.

Now we're outside a bar. Claudia has miraculously found us after being away all day in her frantic world of work. She's wearing a fitted, floor-length dress of psychedelic purple, black and acid green, belted with a big square wooden buckle at the centre of her slightly rounded belly. Her bare arms and shoulders are pale and beautiful, and her long dark hair curls down her back. As she wipes her damp forehead with the back of her hand, I can see she's dying to pull that glossy mass into a sensible, everyday ponytail, but she's determined to be beautiful tonight.

Claudia's brought some friends with her, Sami and Luke, a golden couple who are the conduit for Esther's drugs, but also her enemies. Sami and Esther have played tag team with a couple of boyfriends, and it's all been a bit ugly. Both women are smart and beautiful and studying medicine; each can't stand the Queen Bee status of the other. No room is big enough for the both of them, yet Claudia persists in bringing them together, almost as if she likes to watch the air crackle and pop with the imminent, though never actual, catfight between them.

Sami's small and dark, with the Asian eyes her mother gave her and the broad, high cheekbones of her Danish father. She wears her black hair in a Betty Boop bob and her perfect olive skin is all on show except for a tiny, electric-blue halter dress. The way it ties at the neck reminds me of kindergarten playgrounds and cut lunches; all of a sudden I want to play with her, be her friend, hang upside down on the monkey bars with her and tell her my secrets. I can see that she feels the same way about me as she takes my hand, giggles and says, 'Claudia's told me all about you, naughty girl.'

Flushed and happy, Claudia grabs both of us by the shoulder, telling us we'll get along 'like a house on fire'. Esther scowls, then disappears to try to talk our way past the bouncers into the bar.

I look up at Luke, who's standing like a handsome blond mannequin, dumbly watching his girlfriend in action. Six foot three, he's a pillar of lean, tanned muscle. Isaac is trying to make conversation with him, but Luke is silent and motionless, except for the way he keeps pushing his straight, gold-streaked hair out of his eyes.

'Don't worry about Luke,' says Sami conspiratorially to Isaac and me. 'He's just vain and rude, and he's had too much of something tonight.' She looks up at him and runs her hand along his biceps, which he flexes slightly. 'He did push-ups before we came out, to pump himself up.' Luke smiles and shrugs; he doesn't care that we know about his vanity. 'He's such a girl,' says Sami, 'but he's so beautiful I forgive him.' At this she starts to kiss him, for a long, long time, and we look away.

Soon we're all in the Irish-themed bar, waiting for midnight. The windows are open onto the street, but it's still a closed venue, so we're lucky to get in. The band isn't bad and the girls serving drinks behind the counter are slick with competence, pumping them out. There's one with the strongest brown arms and she's magnificent; I can't stop watching her. She's in a tight leather vest and knows what she's doing, almost without looking. Muscles and leather and unruly hair. Is she gay? Maybe that's why she treats the men with such casual disdain. Or maybe this is her way of keeping their eyes from tearing her apart and making her lose her balance.

The jostling is almost unbearable. There's the stink of spilt beer and sweat and too much expensive Christmas-present perfume. Claudia orders glass after glass of Scotch and Coke, while Esther and I sneer at her. After years of teenage prohibition, we've bypassed such sweet concoctions, together with the milky drinks we started on. We pretend to like our drinks clear and sour now, and think we're superior because of it – but really, we all just want to get drunk.

There's a moment just before midnight when everything seems right between me and Isaac. The band is playing 'Mustang Sally' with its hard, addictive beat. The easy lyrics cry out to be remembered and sung; Isaac is growling along with Joe Cocker and looking at me. His hair is loose and his lips look red against his just-been-ill skin. He's dancing with his body pressed into my back, lending me his rhythm and his protection against the surging crowd.

Esther's dancing too and her silver-clad bottom draws our eyes downwards. She's moving between her English friends and us. For a few seconds, Isaac and Esther and I are a laughing, swaying threesome. They move easily together, and their voices are happy and loud in my ears. They tug me along and I feel small and loved, the centre of a circle. I smile up at Isaac and pull him down to kiss me. I'm a little bit drunk and I don't mind who sees me in love with my husband, pushing my tongue into a mouth that tastes as sweet and familiar and satisfying as cold milk.

And then it's midnight, and everybody's kissing and hugging. Claudia rushes over to us with Sami and Luke, and we're all in a swirling world of love. Just for a minute.

But after the midnight kisses are wantonly distributed, Isaac turns sullen once more.

'Can we go home now? I'm tired,' he says.

I'm astonished that he could really think we've had enough. We haven't even started to plunder our packets of magic.

Esther remembers this and grabs my arm, guiding me into the women's toilets. I yell to Isaac to wait outside with the rest of our group. Esther and I crowd into a cubicle and sit on the lid, giggling in the sudden quiet. She rolls a clean new twenty-dollar note into a tube and sifts a little white powder onto the shiny surface of my red leather wallet. I watch in fascinated horror at the incongruity of a beautiful woman snorting and snuffling in a grotty loo. I follow her lead and feel the strange fizz of speed in my nostrils through the sour smell of money. The ecstasy can wait till the next venue.

'I love you, my darling friend,' she says, like an incantation. 'This night is ours.'

'I adore you, my precious soulmate,' I reply.

We sit crouched, holding hands and grinning at each other for a long moment.

Outside, Isaac looks distressed. He says he's really not feeling well.

'Do you want to go home?' I ask.

'Yes,' he says, annoyed. 'I told you that already.'

'Do I *have* to come?' I plead.

'It's up to you.' His voice is tight. 'Do what you want.'

'Do you really mind?' I'm asking for permission, but he won't give it to me. 'Here's the house key,' I say, digging it out of my handbag and pressing it into his pocket.

'I'll just try to find a taxi, then, on my own.' He grabs my eyes with his, begging me to join him. I pretend not to see. A cab pulls up right beside us as if summoned by Esther's wishes, and mine.

I kiss him goodnight with my eyes open, already looking for the next thing. I won't be home for hours and he knows it.

~⌒

Esther waves goodbye to her English friends, who are also heading off to bed. But the rest of us wander up the street to a club. We move slowly through the crowds, which are growing increasingly ugly as the night's heat persists and the promises of midnight have shown themselves false and fragile.

We pass a couple of drunks smashing bottles against a pole and we see a man thrown through an open street-level restaurant window. For a second we think he might be dead, but he gets up and starts to howl with laughter, blood flowing from a gash on his eyebrow. Then a woman runs screaming down the street, dragging a red vinyl handbag as if it's a small dog out for a run; she's followed by a man who's yelling her name and calling her a slut. The Aboriginal people in the park have lit a fire in a drum, and the smoke is drifting up the road, the smell of danger. Police and ambulance sirens layer the air. I feel like I'm caught in a disaster zone.

Claudia and Esther sense my panic. They're used to this territory with its obnoxious customers and lurking dangers, but I'm not. Isaac and I don't go out like this much in Melbourne, and when we do, it's not rough like Perth. My friends each grab one of my arms and tell me just to keep walking. 'Don't look anybody in the eye,' says Claudia. 'We're nearly there.'

Soon we're showing our IDs to the bouncers (at twenty-four we're thrilled to be asked) and walking into a club that feels like a comforting velveteen womb after the hardness outside. It's split into several levels, with separate spaces for dancing and talking and drinking. We set up home in a little alcove with cushions and carpeted benches, laying down our handbags and taking off our shoes. Then we sit and recover, letting our eyes adjust to the dim purple light.

And then, leaving Luke to look after our things, we four girls head off in a gaggle to the ladies' room to swallow the pills that will make us love ourselves until the dawn kicks us out the door.

'They don't look like proper pills,' I say, staring at the crumbling, sand-coloured tablet in my hand, but not knowing what a proper ecstasy pill looks like anyway. 'Where do they come from?'

'Bikies, up in the hills,' says Sami. 'Go on, just take it.'

'Drink lots of water,' says Esther.

We swallow them then, in front of the mirrors above the basins, and try to fill up the water bottles we've brought with us. The stingy management, no longer making profits from drink sales, has turned nasty with the taps, installing sinks that can't accommodate more than one cupped hand. But we're determined to have our water for free. 'It's a human right!' says Claudia defiantly.

We're damp and dripping when we return to our lair. We've splashed water onto our faces and down our breasts, and rubbed it into our arms because there are no towels and the hand-dryers are out of order. The night is still so warm and it feels divine to be wet. We're dry within minutes anyway.

Luke lounges against the wall, long legs and arms making elegant angles that speak of languor and luxury. His eyes are half shut. He's slipped his own pill down his lazy throat, and it's there in his stomach mingling with whatever else he's taken tonight. Sami goes up to him and strokes his cheek, and he rests his big head against her flat chest. He smiles at us, from far away.

Then Sami and Esther run off together to the dance floor, their enmity forgotten for a little while because they both love to dance. Claudia pushes Luke's legs off the bench and flops herself down without pause, gesturing for me to join her. Her movements are big and aggressive – no, they're assertive. I love the way she takes her rights and pastes them up, as if to say that she *will* take up space in this world and to hell with anyone who objects. She lets her breath out loudly and sags against the wall, undoing the belt and throwing it in the corner near our handbags.

'That's better,' she says, sighing deeply. 'I had too much lasagne for dinner. Grabbed it on the run from Granny's when I finished my cleaning job.'

'You're amazing,' I say. 'Cleaning houses on New Year's Eve!'

'It's nothing. Just a couple of hours. And now I've got money for Granny's rates.'

I know that those 'couple of hours' would have seen Claudia with her sweaty rubber-gloved hands in bleach, down on her knees scrubbing the stains from toilet bowls. In this heat she would have been dripping over the vacuum cleaner. Hard slog. She's a good girl, and I feel the guilt of my own laziness; the way I run from hard work, except if there's some glory involved. Or a deadline I can't avoid. 'You make me feel so slack,' I say.

'Rubbish! You're on your holiday. Why should you be working? You study so hard all year.'

This isn't actually true, but I don't correct her. She has an image of me that is shiny and diligent; she remembers me in primary school, head bent over prayers, or in high school staying up all night to polish essays until I could recite them in my head.

'And when are *you* going to take a holiday?' I ask.

'Soon,' she says. 'Well, maybe in a few years, when I've finished my course.' She's going to start studying Property Valuation this year, because that's where the money is; Perth's about to go mental with land prices, everybody says so.

'Don't become a workaholic,' I warn. 'I've hardly seen you, you've been working so hard.'

She leans on my shoulder. 'I know, luvvie. But you've been busy too. Having adventures.' She slurps from her water bottle, then sits up straight, as if realising something's missing. 'Where's Isaac?'

'He wasn't feeling well.'

'Oh, poor baby! I didn't even get to say goodnight to him. Is he going to be okay on his own?'

'Yeah, he'll be fine.' I rest my head back against the carpeted cave and shut my eyes tight on the image of Isaac, pale and alone in the big house. I hope the taxi got him there okay. What I want to say to Claudia is, 'Please don't tell me I should be there with him, giving up my special night to look after him, when really he's just being sulky.' But instead I sigh, stretching my fingers out and scratching my nails down the purple wall in tactile fascination. I want to stroke the dirty carpet and feel its roughness on my palms. I want to chew – I wish I had some gum.

Claudia looks at me closely. 'Are you two going to be okay? You know, your marriage?'

I stare at her as if it's a question I've never really considered before. Last time we spoke about this, when she mentioned the sex counselling, I was so vehement that divorce wasn't an option for us.

'I don't know,' I say.

'Is it about Jay? Do you love Jay?'

'I do love him, but I don't think it's about that.'

'Be careful, precious,' she says. 'Don't throw things away too quickly.'

'But you and Esther were the ones telling me I got married too young and giving up was no shame!'

She shrugs. 'Now he's here and I see you two together, and it's not all bad.'

'I don't know what to do,' I say.

'I don't know anything either,' she says, 'except that I don't want you to be sad. I see that Isaac makes you sad, and he looks sad too. But somehow you belong together.'

I'm having trouble concentrating. Right now there's no

sadness for me, because I'm diving into Claudia's beautiful chocolate fondue eyes. We sit staring at each other until our eyes begin to cross, and then we giggle. Esther and Sami find us like this when they come back from the dance floor, with their faces red and eyes bright.

'I'm starting to feel it,' says Esther, and Sami nods. They both look at me, pushing their foreheads almost against mine. 'Ooh, your pupils are huge,' says Esther. 'Let's go and look at them.'

She takes my hand and together we run off to the bathroom where we stare at our eyes, standing alongside three girls we've never met. They're doing the same thing.

'Beautiful, beautiful,' says Esther, turning to me.

Now we're staring at each other, and all the boundaries between us are dissolving. Her eyes are icy-blue crystals around black pools and I think she might be me, and I might be her, and this smile she's giving me is actually an extension of the one I'm giving her. Do we share one mind?

Then we're kissing.

I've kissed a couple of girls before, but Esther hasn't and she's delighted at the threshold she's crossed. 'I'm so glad it's with you,' she says, looking into my eyes again. Her giant pupils are holes I could fall into. I love that I can take her somewhere she's never been before, lead her down a path like she's done for me so many times.

Her lips are so, *so* soft and her breath is sweet with peppermint chewing gum, and I'm thinking that I've looked at these lips a million times. I've watched them talk and laugh and smoke. I've seen her wrinkle them in horror and I've seen them crumple when her heart's been broken. I've loved to look at them pursed in front of the mirror applying lip gloss since we were nine years old. These are the dearest lips in the world, and I've never touched them before with my own.

'You're a lovely kisser,' she says as she breaks away, and we giggle, because when we were growing up we used to worry that we wouldn't know how to kiss; that there might be some secret technique that everyone else knew.

'You're a wonderful kisser too,' I say. 'Let's do it again.'

So we do, braver now, putting our tongues in. And then we join hands and move back outside, grinning from ear to ear. Claudia and Sami are watching us emerge, and they see that we're changed, that we've come back with something we didn't have before we went in. Then we start kissing in front of them, partly to show them what we're so happy about, but also because we don't want to stop. It's silk, it's velvet, it's suede and it's sweet. It's pink and gentle and smells like gardenia.

Sami's coming over and she's kissing the back of my neck. Then Sami and Esther are kissing, their eyes open, and I wonder if it's a truce or a rivalrous challenge. Sami grabs my hand and pulls me closer to her, away from Esther. She's grinning like a little Cheshire cat, and then her lips are on mine, and I'm running my fingers through that black hair, and down that hot skin on her back that reminds me of smooth blanched almonds.

I look over at Luke, who's watching us with a slow smile. Sami pushes me towards him. 'Kiss him if you want. Try him, he's gorgeous.' So I do. And it's true, he's divinely beautiful. I love the muscles of his long body and the flatness of his stomach. The smell of his aftershave reminds me of old wood and pine needles. But he seems so far away from reality. It feels like kissing a phantom, a shadow, a dream of a man who can't quite make you come before you wake up.

Claudia's watching us all with bemusement and mild disgust. 'Do whatever you want to,' she says, 'but I'm not kissing anybody. So don't come near me if that's what you're after.'

We tease her and prod her, but there's no way she's joining in. We don't really mind, though I would love to feel those large, soft breasts squashed against mine. She's only taken half a pill because she's our caretaker tonight, our prim governess, and we're glad there's an adult in charge.

Esther leads me down to the bar area, where the music is louder and the lights are pinker. She wants us to have some time alone, to test our togetherness on the rest of the world. Or maybe she wants to get me away from Sami. We kiss in front of a guy who's watching us, grabbing each other's arses and making a show of it. We let him join in for a while. I kiss his neck while she's on his lips and then we swap. But he's crass and he smells of beer. 'I'll have you sitting on my face,' he says, kissing me on the nose, 'and you sucking my cock', to Esther as he goes to nuzzle her neck.

She pulls away with a grimace. 'Oh, we don't like that. Do we, Eve?'

'No, we don't like that,' I say, shaking my head like a displeased child.

'Come on, you're up for it. You want it.' He's begging now. 'You two need a *man*.'

'No, we don't, actually,' says Esther. 'We want to play on our own.' She pulls me away and we walk off holding hands and whispering.

'Lesbian cunts,' he mutters, but we're too happy with each other to respond.

'I'd love for us to have a bath together,' says Esther, as she gently pushes me against a wall and kisses my throat. 'Baths are so great on E.'

'Why don't we, then?' I shove my hands down the back of her pants and feel the thread of her G-string. I'm thinking about being in the bath with her. The fun we could have.

'What, go home now?' she says.

'We could.'

'Okay. Let's. Soon.'

But the hours dissolve in the soft steam of music and dancing and kissing. Before we know it, the club's shutting and it's time for us to leave. It's 5am and the sun is just coming up. The streets are still hot and dirty, but there's a morning freshness. After five hours of drumbeat, the quiet is a shock. A taxi scrolls around the corner, as if we've scripted it, and Esther and Claudia and I scramble in, with quick goodbyes to Sami and Luke. 'Happy New Year!' we scream out the windows and it echoes down the deserted street. We don't stop waving until they're out of sight.

The cab is gathering speed now. We're leaving the city, driving south across the Swan River. All of a sudden, as we ascend the causeway bridge, the sun is blasting down and turning the water into a sparkling cluster of diamonds that wink and twinkle with a brilliance that's friendly and spectacular all at once. Esther sees it too, and she sighs happily. She holds on to my arm and says, 'Look at the river, Eve, look at the river, Clauds. The new year's really begun!'

Claudia's got her head back and her eyes shut. 'I've seen it all before,' she says, refusing to open them. 'I'm so sick of the bloody river. All I want to see now is clean sheets and a hot shower.'

But Esther and I can't take our eyes off the morning. It's too beautiful, too blue and gold and speedy for sleep.

'It's 1997,' I say, with wonder.

'We didn't even make any resolutions,' she says, disappointed. 'We have to do that.'

'I can't wait for our bath. I need a bath.'

'Not long now,' she says as the taxi cruises into her street, past the neat lawns with sprinklers just coming in, and the cream and red double-brick houses. 'After our bath we'll play music and put on silk dressing-gowns. They *have* to be silk. Then we'll lie under the fan and make our resolutions.'

Out of the taxi, we fumble with the door key and stumble into the hot, stuffy house. Esther suddenly lurches into the kitchen and grabs the sink, splashing her face with water. She slides down to the floor and puts her face on the cool white tiles, which are not entirely clean.

'Oh, oh, oh!' she moans. 'I feel so sick.'

'Honey, honey,' says Claudia, rushing over. 'How many tablets did you have?'

Esther looks up pleadingly. 'I took the spare one too,' she says in a small voice. 'The one we got for Isaac.'

'You silly, greedy girl.' Claudia feels Esther's forehead, which looks pink and sweaty.

'I think I'm going to throw up,' says Esther. And Claudia guides her quickly to the bathroom down the hallway, from where I can hear her ministrations between Esther's groans: 'Honey, just let it all out. Oh, you've got some in your hair. Here, jump in the shower.'

Thank god for Claudia. She's on watch. My first and greatest feeling is sadness that Esther and I won't be having our bath anymore, that our trip together is over so suddenly. I'm speeding now, and chewing desperately on a piece of gum as if my jaw will collapse and crush all my teeth if I stop. I walk into the lounge room and lie on the carpet, holding a plush cushion to my cheek.

Claudia comes out and says she's going to sleep beside Esther to keep an eye on her and make sure she's breathing, so there's no need to worry.

I hear this from a great distance. The worry I felt about Esther's health rises up into the exposed beams of the ceiling. I lie there awake, more awake than I've ever been in my life, but so still, except for the chewing, which makes a rhythmic squeak that I breathe along to. I don't move for hours.

Then the gathering heat sends me upstairs to the air-conditioned bedroom where Isaac sleeps. As I walk in, I realise that I haven't even checked on him since I got home. Is he breathing? I flop onto the bed and rest my head on his chest to make sure of it.

He pushes me away. 'You stink! Go and have a shower.'

So I do. A long and soapy daze. When I come back to bed, naked and damp, and gingerly climb in beside him, he reaches out of his semi-sleep, grabs my hand and gently holds it to his heart. 'Are you okay?' he murmurs. 'What did you take?'

'Speed. Ecstasy.'

'Idiot!' He's cross. 'Just try to sleep now, or at least let me get some.' There's gruff kindness in his voice, relief that I'm back. I can't tell how much trouble I'm going to be in when we emerge later on. How much trouble will I be in for abandoning him, for taking illegal substances, for kissing so many friends and strangers that I can't even count them right now?

I will be in trouble, but I'll be forgiven, I know. I lie listening to his breath and wishing that there was some logic that would satisfy him as to why I am as I am, and why I've done what I've done. But there is none, and I regret nothing.

12

It's early afternoon on New Year's Day when we all surface from sleep – or, in my case, from dozing in and out of speedy dreams – to face the white heat. Esther looks pale and tired as she slowly makes tea in the kitchen. I set out the cups on the bench for her, and she comes over to me and croaks, 'Hug?'

I wrap my arms around her gently, and we rock from side to side. I kiss her soft, smooth cheek and wonder if there'll be awkwardness after last night: her tongue in my mouth, my hand down the back of her pants, and the desire we felt to be alone in the bath with our fingers inside each other, or was that just where my dirty mind was leading us? It all feels like a faraway dream now. I smile at her and she smiles back with a laugh at the corners of her eyes, where crinkles are just starting to form. Nothing has changed. What happened last night is just another point on the continuum of our naughtiness: getting drunk on cask wine at fourteen, or masturbating side by side as we read aloud the Harlequin romances stolen from her sister's room.

Isaac and Claudia are in the lounge room fiddling with the air-conditioning unit, which refuses to crank up. Isaac's hair clings damply to his forehead and Claudia is cursing as she balances on a stool and bangs the brown plastic casing that should be blowing cold air. 'It's too fucking hot in here!' she shouts. 'Work, you piece of shit!'

'Ouch, too loud!' Esther says, adding, 'Somebody's going to have to collect the car we left in South Perth last night.'

'*Your* car,' says Claudia, who seems to have run out of sympathy after nursing Esther's overdose all night.

'I can't leave the house in this heat or I'll pass out.' Esther flops down in a chair as she says this, to prove that even the strength to stand up is deserting her.

'Isaac and I will go,' I say, looking over at him and silently begging him to accept the mission. 'We'll take Claudia's car and I'll drive back Esther's. We're not *too* seedy …'

'I'm not seedy at all,' says Isaac pointedly. 'But Eve might not even pass a breath test – or whatever it is they use to check you for drugs.'

I shut my eyes tight as if to block out his judgement. There'll be more to come, and I'm dreading it. I'm still speeding. He feels so heavy and I want to be light.

~⌒~

We're in Claudia's little old car now: a box of bottled heat, smelling of chewing gum. I find half a packet wedged near the gear stick and pop two pellets into my mouth. Chewing feels so good that I want more bulk to chomp on, so I squeeze a couple more pellets straight onto my tongue.

Isaac looks over at me from the driver's seat. 'You take too much, you know that?'

'*So* excessive, four pieces of chewie!'

'What happened last night then, after I left?' he asks.

'A club. Some dancing, some *frolicking*.' Chew, chew. I want another one.

'What kind of frolicking?'

'Y'know. We had the tablets. It was touchy-feely. Smoochy.'

'Smoochy? Like kissing?' He frowns when I nod. 'With who?'

'A couple of people.'

I look out the window as we're heading down the street where Esther's car should be parked. Please God, let it be in the shade of one of these gum trees. Please let the windows not be smashed in. There it is – I see it in the distance, the little white Corolla, intact and innocent-seeming. It looks heartbreakingly alone, parked there a lifetime ago.

'Just up on the left,' I say, pointing, and Isaac pulls in behind, keeping the engine running but putting the gearstick into 'park'. I guess he wants to talk, but I'm keen to get out and drive home separately as quickly as possible. I unbuckle my seatbelt and open the door.

'Wait,' he says. 'A couple of people? Who?'

'Esther's friends, Sami and Luke ... and Esther?' My voice trails upwards at the end.

'Right.' He keeps his eyes straight ahead. 'Esther? Esther. What are you doing, Eve?'

I look down at my hands, fiddle with my rings and say very softly, 'Just playing.' There's silence, so I add, 'Isn't that what we're all about?'

'Don't be so disingenuous, pretending you're not breaking our rules.'

'But why do we have to even have rules?' I ask. 'It doesn't work in the real world if I have to ask you everything first, when I don't even know what I'm going to do next … It's not spontaneous.'

'It's called *marriage*, Eve. I don't ask for much, just to be consulted.' He takes a deep breath, and I can hear it's ragged with anger. 'You can't even do that, can you?'

I think for a moment about how he's reacting, the feeling of betrayal he has because I kissed a few people while on New Year's Eve drugs. He doesn't even know about Marcus and Peter, and about how close I'm getting to Jay. The weight of all these secrets makes me sick in the pit of my stomach, so I push them down into the dark again; perhaps they didn't happen if I don't think about them.

'You're the one who went home early on New Year's Eve,' I say, drawing a winning point out of the air. 'I wanted you there, remember? You could have been part of it all. We would have had fun. Together. Like we used to.'

'I was sick, for god's sake. I needed you to come home with me.'

'I'm sorry,' I say, and at that moment I feel it, like nausea.

'Are you? Are you really sorry?'

I reach over and put my hand on the back of his neck the way I often do when he's driving, finding the hollow at the base of his hairline and placing my finger in it for a tiny, deep massage. 'I love you,' I say, and I feel the truth of that bubbling up with the power of the words.

'I love you too, bad wife,' he says with a small laugh. But he looks so sad I can hardly bear it.

I move to open the door, but he pulls me back by my wrist, leaning in for a kiss. His lips touch mine. And then he says, 'I'm glad I'm going to have you to myself tonight.'

Ah, now I remember. We're booked into a hotel overlooking the sea, a luxury suite as a treat for our final night in Perth. Isaac insisted on this when we planned the trip, saying that he wanted to make sure we had some time on our own. Away from Esther, he meant.

I grin. 'I can't wait to get there – air conditioning! And we can swim in the ocean at sunset.'

'Isn't that when the sharks come out?' he asks.

I picture him pale and afraid in the waves, and immediately know it's not going to happen.

'Well, we can get room service and watch the sunset from our balcony. And then you can spend all night watching cable TV.' I poke my tongue out at him. 'Like you did on our wedding night.'

'It wasn't *all* night,' he protests. 'That night was great.'

It's true. It was great. We'd driven away from the ghastly wedding with such haste and glee, so eager to have our first night alone, really alone, sleeping together without any fear of being found out. Shutting the door on the world in the Rockman's Regency that cold July night, we'd looked at each other and laughed. Suddenly we weren't just allowed to be alone, and naked, but we were *supposed* to be. All those guests at the sober wedding were imagining us doing it. This seemed so grotesque that we almost wanted to wait for days to 'consummate' in order to spite them.

But after the spa bath had washed away the confetti stuck down my cleavage, and the chocolates had been eaten off our pillows, we'd had the exhausted, lazy sex of two happy people unaccustomed to complimentary champagne and privacy. When I'd fallen asleep to the sound of Isaac watching television, it had felt like blissful safety; like someone keeping watch while I gave myself up to unconsciousness. I knew he'd be there in the morning, and every morning afterwards.

And here we are four and a half years later, hoping to find our way back to a place like that.

'I can't wait.' He grins as I leave the hot car. 'Let's pick up our stuff from Esther's as soon as we can and get over there quickly. We'll check in before we lose too much more of the day.'

The sun is already low in the sky by the time we check in to Observation City, the hotel by the sea. Perth's most famous millionaire, Alan Bond, built it back in the eighties amid protest from the locals. It still stands out like a sore thumb on the Scarborough foreshore, making the mighty Norfolk pines look puny. Twenty-four stories high, it's a cream-coloured concrete tower that taste forgot.

We step out of the mirrored lift on the tenth floor, feet sinking into thick carpet as we find our way down the amber-lit corridor. So many doors, so many rooms – all occupied. 'A full house tonight,' we were told at reception by a pimply young concierge, who seemed proud of having no vacancies. Yet there are so few signs of life in this crowded mini-city built on the sand.

I suddenly think of the jaunty song we used to sing in Sabbath School, the one based on Christ's parable about the two houses: one built on rock and one on sand. Making provisions for eternal life, that was the whole purpose of our childhood education. But now all I want is to feel a succession of moments with my feet shifting under me, according to the movement of the waves.

'Think of all the sex that goes on behind these doors,' I whisper as we stand in the recessed entry, while Isaac fiddles with the room key.

'Think of all the people paying five hundred dollars a night,' he says loudly, refusing to be cowed by the velvety silence. 'Spending seventy cents a minute for the privilege of stiff sheets and stale air.' The key clicks into the lock, finally. 'Do you reckon there's much good fucking going on with all that pressure on them?' He likes to sound cynical and world-weary, but I know he loves the anonymous luxury of big hotels even more than I do.

'Seventy cents a minute? Did you just work that out in your head?'

'It's only rough.'

'Well, I hope we get our money's worth.' I smile up at him as he holds the door open for me.

'It's worth it just for the peace,' he says, and I wonder silently if either one of us will have the energy or the inclination for anything more than sleep. I certainly don't feel like it.

I move quickly through the gloom to the other side of the room, ripping back the peach-coloured double drapes that hem in the space and mask the balcony doors. I want to go outside to get my bearings, so I slide open the door and stand on the small ledge facing south towards Fremantle, the ocean on my right. The balcony is too shallow to fit a table or chairs, just an ashtray stashed tidily in the corner for errant smokers.

Out over the water there's the start of a muted sunset, hazy with low-lying clouds. The air still vibrates with heat, despite the wind blowing up from the beach. I feel the stickiness of salt in the air, coating my skin and gritting my spirit. There's a dirty heaviness I can't shake, even as I look down at the perfect Indian Ocean. It's always lifted my mood, but the magic's not working today, which I guess is my body's payback for all the poison I put into it last night.

'Come and see the sun slip into the ocean!' I call back through the doorway.

I imagine Isaac emerging to stand behind me, wrapping his arms around me as we watch it together in a parody of romance. I'd like to lean back and feel him there, keeping my balance.

'Quick, it's about to happen!' I yell.

'Just give me a minute to work out the remote.'

I can hear the concentration in his voice. He's sitting on the edge of the bed, skimming through cable options, pausing at the porn teasers and the action trailers. Technology and its screens are always so much safer and more enticing to him than nature. My nature, in particular.

I watch alone as the yolk of the sun sinks into the silent, hazy horizon. The golden light gives way to darkness almost immediately and I shut my eyes, wishing I could feel something meaningful or memorable. Something deserving of nature's show. But I'm blank.

There's a slap on my neck, sharp and sudden. 'Mozzie!' Isaac's holding up a finger smeared with blood and a squashed, spindle-legged corpse. 'Did I miss the sunset?' he asks vaguely.

'Never mind. It wasn't that great.'

'You should come inside anyway, before you're mozzie meat. Want to watch a movie?'

'I need a bath first,' I say, thinking of the coolness of a large marble tub and longing to be rid of the grimy layer on my skin. 'Why don't you have one with me?'

'You start. I might come in later.' He takes off his t-shirt and jeans, stripping down to faded red underpants. He throws his long, narrow body down on the king-size bed, spreading his arms and legs out like a starfish and grinning at me. 'The space! I can't even touch the sides.' He moves his limbs in and out as if making snow angels. 'I want us to get one of these beds, darling. Can we?'

'Of course we can. But would it fit in our bedroom?'

'Good point.' He adjusts the pillows against the beige satin headrest and starts flicking through the channels again. 'Go on, put lots of bubbles in. I'll bring you a drink in a minute.'

I shut the bathroom door to block out the noise from the television, and turn the golden taps on to full stream so the water pounds into the tub. The cold cream tiles feel good on my hot feet as I shed my faded floral sundress and let it pool on the floor, a flimsy ghost. The light's too bright, with too many mirrors reflecting my image on three walls. Too much of that girl. I'm sick of her. She's wearing a white bra with grimy straps and black lace underpants that were once part of a fancy set – the careless coordination of a hung-over slattern. Her face is pale from lack of sleep, dark hair pulled back into a spiky ponytail that glows red under the gold lights. She leans in closer to the mirror to see if her pupils are still dilated, but her eyes are dull and regular again.

In this windowless room, the lighting choice seems to be between glaring fluorescence and total blackness. I long for the forgiving flicker of a candle, a single tea-light, but then I make

do with the globes that are studded around the vanity mirror –
a dim yellow halo designed to inform each hotel guest that just
for today, as long as they're paying, they're a movie star waiting
to be made up.

I crack open the paper jacket on a disc of hotel soap. It's
smooth in my hand like a creamy stone. I sniff the miniature
bottle of bubble bath: astringent and rosemary-scented in an
artificial way; it will have to do. I empty the gloopy gel into
the water where it instantly billows into fragrant white foam,
and I wonder, vaguely, if the real purpose of a bubble bath is to
cover the surface of the water, so a person can avoid seeing the
submerged mass of their ugly flesh.

I slide with relief beneath the foam, suddenly weightless,
letting my head sink back into the soapy water so that just my
nose and mouth are exposed. Bubbles cling to my cheeks and I
can hear the pop of them and the amplified drip of the tap.

The bath is so big and deep that I can almost float. And
I think of all the floating I've done in the past weeks – the
fevered time-machine fuck with my first love, then drifting
into a date-rape-turned-pleasure-cruise with Peter. And
falling, falling, falling for Jay in our sleepless week of fighting
and fucking and telling the truth, the whole truth, until I felt
fully naked.

I want Jay. I wonder where he's been these last twenty-
four hours and how his own New Year's panned out. It's
late at night in Melbourne, so he's probably awake. I want
to tell him about last night. About me and Esther and the
softness of her skin. Me and Sami and the way her cat's grin
was fluorescent in the purple light as I traced the bones of her
spine down to her arse. I want to describe Luke for him; he'd

like that. The lazy, impersonal way Luke's eyes slid off mine after we'd kissed.

And I want to tell Jay about the blue, blue sky this morning as we crossed the causeway bridge in the taxi; the way the sun flashed on the water as it shone into the first day of 1997, making me feel free and limitless, as if I might fly up into the horizon and look down on the whole wide Swan River snaking out below me, like at the end of *Cloudstreet*. It wasn't just the drugs. Or maybe it was.

I sit up in the tub and run more hot water into the mix. The air conditioning is fierce, turning the room into a freezer. Isaac will like it, but I want to be warm again, hot again.

The bubbles are dissipating and I see my red-tipped toes wriggling like sea creatures, and the dark seaweed drifting at my groin pulls me into another wish to have Jay here right now. He'd sit outside the tub with his hands dipped into the water, searching for me and playing with me, while we'd carry on a conversation that had nothing to do with his fingers slipping inside me. I let my own fingers play there, imagining they're his, though I haven't the energy for an orgasm right now.

I need to speak to Jay, but I'll have to wait until tomorrow when I can find a moment alone for a phone call before the flight. Maybe there'll be a chance at the airport. I fantasise briefly about making some excuse to go down to the lobby tonight and make a secret call to him. But that would be cheating.

~✎

'Come here, wet woman,' Isaac says, looking over his glasses at me as I stand in the doorway, a fluffy white towel wrapped around me and bubbles still popping against my arms and chest. 'You never dry yourself properly,' he adds, annoyed.

'It's too much effort!' I collapse backwards onto the bed, leaving wet patches on the stiff white sheets.

Isaac turns off the television and leans down to kiss my damp forehead. 'You're all limp and flollopy. You had the water too hot again, didn't you?' He smiles. (Did he coin the word 'flollopy'? Or did we hear it somewhere and adopt it into the lingo of our marriage, along with so many other childish words?) 'Look at you, you're poached! And you wonder why I never get in the bath with you.'

'I thought you were at least going to bring me a drink.'

'Sorry. I forgot. Want one now? Champagne?'

'Ugh. I couldn't. Is there any orange juice?'

He squats down by the bar fridge, peering into it, his white face illuminated by the blue light. I look at him and think how often that face has been turned away from me, illuminated by other light sources, screens that shone more brightly than I ever could. The fights we've had as he's been hunched over the computer. I've been so jealous of his obsessions; I wanted to be the thing that lit him up. 'Find your own obsessions and passions,' he'd said, over and over. 'Have your own adventures.'

So I did – and still, it felt as though all I wanted was for him to look at me.

We watch a movie and then it's late, and the half-eaten room service meal of steak and chips sits on a silver tray on the floor. Scrunched linen napkins cover the leftovers. We should put the tray outside the door to be collected by the invisible ants that run the hotel, but we're lazy and sleepy, so the room smells of grease.

The bed is hard and unyielding and, like in all hotel rooms, there aren't nearly enough pillows. Isaac's taken my share to prop him up for reading. My head's resting on his chest instead. The bedside lamp is switched on beside him, but my side is dark. I have the flat, dread-filled feeling of coming down off the drugs, desperately craving sleep but unable to achieve it.

I listen to his heartbeat and feel myself rise and fall with his breath, as I have on so many other sleepless nights. I wonder what it might be like to live without this steady thump of warmth beneath my cheek. Could I do it?

Sensing I'm awake, he strokes my hair. 'Can't sleep?'

'Can't stop my brain.'

'Speed will do that to you, idiot,' he says, but kindly. 'Hey, I forgot. I brought us something special. It might help.'

He goes over to his suitcase in the corner and pulls something from beneath a mess of clothes. He holds it up with a grin and I see that it's the last book in the series we've been reading together, *The House at Pooh Corner*. I've loved to have Isaac read these silly, sweet books aloud to me before bedtime – loved to hear the precise ways of the orator that he's never embarrassed to use.

I never read AA Milne's books as a child, because they lack the plot and obvious moralising that my parents required for my carefully selected Christian library. Even the allegories of *The Chronicles of Narnia* felt slightly illicit, because their magic was questionably pagan. Mum didn't like them at all, though I persisted. But Isaac's Anglophile mother added classics to her children's library, putting Milne and Beatrix Potter and Lewis Carroll onto the shelves right up close to the same bible books I'd had.

Isaac has shared all his favourites with me over this last year, in a bedtime ritual that's bound us together, brought us back into harmony even when I've returned from outings with Jay. We've made the Winnie the Pooh series last, rationing it out like sweets to be devoured before sleep; honey and milk to make our dreams gentle. We've kept ourselves from reading this final precious chapter until the last possible moment. And here it is, this night that was supposed to feel like a honeymoon.

I settle into the crook of his arm again and close my eyes. Isaac begins, and I'm lulled by the English nursery logic. Here we are again with the Bear of Very Little Brain, the Rabbit with all his relations, and Eeyore and Piglet, and Christopher Robin who's being delightful and wise. It's so familiar and comforting – and as Isaac's reading to me, it's all coming to an end in the Enchanted Wood, because Christopher Robin has to go off into the world by himself (to school?) and learn about 'Kings and Queens and something called Factors, and a place called Europe, and an island in the middle of the sea where no ships came, and how you make a Suction Pump (if you want to), and when Knights were Knighted, and what comes from Brazil'.

I listen with my eyes wide open now. My cheek is growing hot with dread against Isaac's pumping heart. He keeps on reading as the Bear of Very Little Brain is made a Faithful Knight, and wonders if being a Faithful Knight means going on being faithful, even when you're not being told things anymore, even when the love has grown away. '"Pooh," said Christopher Robin earnestly, "if I – if I'm not quite –" he stopped and tried again – "Pooh, *whatever* happens, you *will* understand, won't you?"'

And suddenly, Isaac's voice is full of tears and he's trying to read the last paragraph about somewhere 'a little boy and his Bear will always be playing', but he can hardly get the words out. My sobs are racking me now. We're holding each other and saying that we don't know why we're so sad. And then we're laughing and kissing, small kisses all over our faces to lick up the tears, not passionate, but like puppies, confused and trying to comfort a huge and overwhelming grief.

'Stupid book.' Isaac laughs, snorting up snot theatrically, pushing the book onto the floor.

But somewhere deep inside the comfort of our air-conditioned room, we know that something's left us. Our garden where we lived on love alone is gone, and not even these wedding rings, which still gleam so brightly, can open the gate that's shut now.

The light has departed from us, and we are so naked and alone.

In the grey flickering of the television we fall into fitful sleep, holding on to each other as if we're on a precipice.

13

I wake early and it takes me a moment to remember where I am. The red numbers on the digital display beside the bed declare 5.20am. The room is cold. In the night I've pulled up the blankets. On Isaac's side they're pushed down to the foot of the bed, where his bony toes rest innocently in a tangle.

I lie on my side looking at him, our faces so close I can smell the faint tang of Scotch on his breath. I fancy that if I focus hard enough, the force of my gaze might wake him up. Then we can talk – not about anything serious, but just because I want another presence to echo my bright wakefulness. I want to hear his voice after the loneliness of the night.

He sleeps on. Lazy red mouth slightly open, dark stubble on his chin, and pallid eyelids fluttering as if in dreams he's lost to me. I want to bring him back. So I run a fingernail along his arm from the elbow to the wrist, digging in a little deeply where his hand rests on the pillow beside his face. He just shrugs me off with a murmur and turns over.

I wonder if it's too early to go for a swim or take a run along the beach. Will the sun be up yet? I can't tell through the drapes, but I guess it won't be long before it's light. My body aches from lack of exercise these last few weeks. In a matter of hours I'll be scrunched into a plane seat, cramped and motionless. I want to move and sweat, like an itch that's becoming unbearable.

In the grey light I rummage around in my suitcase, pulling everything out into a heap until I find my bathers and some denim shorts to wear over the top. White rubber thongs on my feet, I grab a towel and my phone, stealing silently out into the corridor, where it could be any time of the day or night, except for the freshly folded *West Australian* newspaper lying on every doormat. I leave the paper inside the door for Isaac to find when he wakes, imagining him turning straight to the weather forecast and the comics. He'll smile while he gulps his instant coffee from the shallow, thick-lipped teacups on top of the minibar.

As the lift descends I try not to see myself in the mirrored walls, but can't help noticing that my eyes are still puffy from last night's crying. I shut them tight and lean back against the wall, tired at the memory of the weeping. The cold sea water will do me good.

The concierge at the desk smiles wearily as I pass. He must be nearing the end of his shift; there are dark shadows on his jaw and his white collar's not quite fresh. The automatic doors part in front of me and I exit like a queen gliding out into the dawn, where the light is just starting to turn into muted, cloudy gold. The air feels fresher than it's been for days, but still warmer than inside the hotel. Perhaps the heatwave will break today. But those frivolous clouds in the distance bear no rain.

The beach isn't nearly as empty as I'd expected. There's a sprinkling of keen joggers fulfilling New Year's exercise resolutions. They dot the hard-packed wet sand close to the shoreline as I look south towards Freo and north up to Trigg. In front of me a lone swimmer wades out thigh-deep, his large brown belly unashamed above red budgie-smugglers. He has to wade some distance to get fully wet, but when he gets there, where the waves are breaking, they're big enough to give a satisfying crash. He disappears into the wash, ducking and diving like a plump seal.

Brownish-green seaweed lies in tidy clumps along the shoreline, as if the sea has swept them up but forgotten the dustpan. Apart from these, the beach looks wide and clean and pure, the way a beach should look. The way it never looks around the cramped and dirty bay in Melbourne, where the sea air smells like old fish and industrial waste. Even that thought feels like a guilty jab at Isaac.

Breathing in deeply, salt air tingling in my nostrils, I think of my mother and the way she always advised us to 'breathe in those positive ions' whenever we were by the ocean. She had to make even a pleasure trip to the beach into a health tonic. And the truth is that, despite being naughty on special occasions, I'm like my parents in this way – a helpless health fanatic. Already I can feel the sea air doing me good, and I want to make the most of this wholesome hour. I want to atone for the unaccustomed drugs and alcohol that are still leaving my system.

I find a hollow in the shallow dunes and leave my towel wrapped around my phone and thongs, half buried in the seagrass, and hope that early morning exercisers are more honest and less prone to theft than most people.

Down on the wet sand I start to run, feeling silly and awkward at first, but gathering ease as I find my rhythm, bare

feet slapping the shore, waves meeting my ankles at uneven
intervals. The sun rises gloriously on my left, casting long, lean
shadows over to my right where the water sparkles and flashes
as it teases the blond sand. I love the look of my shadow, those
spidery legs and arms on a graceful giantess. She races beside
me. We're joined at my feet until we're both out of breath and
ready to turn around. I walk back, my lungs aching and my
face hot and red, but it's all good.

Reaching the spot where my towel and thongs are buried,
I sink onto my knees facing the ocean, my feet splayed out at
either side, toes digging into the cool dry sand, and lie back
from the waist, shutting my eyes against the rising glare. I can
hear the quiet music of a separate universe down there in the
dunes, a gentle breeze whispering and moaning in the grass
away from the dominant crash of waves and the shriek of
seagulls. Sitting up, I look down at those waves that are now
quite high, high enough to scare me as they roll in – pale green,
rearing up taller than a person and crashing pitilessly into
whiteness. Again and again and again.

Just to scare myself, I imagine what a dark-finned shape
would look like in that green glass wave, the one rising up
in front of me with a lazy curl of its lip. Have I seen a photo
like this – a huge black fish suspended in aqua gel, seen by the
photographer, but not by the surfer who shares the wave? I feel
the fear of what lurks beneath at Perth beaches, so notorious for
shark attacks close to shore.

I really don't want to swim alone. But I know I'll hate
myself later if I miss this one last chance. So I walk down to the
water and launch myself into the waves, gasping at the shock of
the cold and diving under the crest of a monster just before it's

about to break. It crashes high over my head, but I'm safe in a little ball. I feel myself spewed back to shore in a swirl of froth and bubbles and grit. It's delicious, a rough caress by a careless beast, and I want to do it again.

I remember the thrill of bodysurfing with my dad when I was nine, ten, eleven at Trigg, 'our beach' just north of here. He must have been about thirty-five then, strong and handsome, and pushing me to be fearless. He always wanted me to be brave. He expected it – with water, waves and sun, anyway. He'd tell me just the right moment to catch the wave, pushing me ahead a little so I had a run on it. And then I could feel the wave at my back and shoulders, where it would carry me, lift me, drive me to the shore like a well-shot dart.

There were times when it didn't work, and I'd be smashed into the underwater basement, ground into the sand with salt water injected up through my nostrils towards my screaming brain, unsure I'd make it to the surface in time to breathe. And then, after a moment in the world of air again, spluttering and relieved to be alive, I'd find Dad's tall figure in the glare beside me, and he'd be laughing at me, unworried. He was so pagan at the beach, as if he was finally set free from religion. He'd shout at me to go again, even though my mother, on the dry sand far away, was gesturing us to come in, it was too dangerous. I'd ignore her and go back out. Because I wanted to, just like now.

I suddenly remember a rare moment alone with my dad, sitting beside him in the back seat of the white Jaguar, my satin wedding dress spread out around me and the smell of red roses filling the car. As we drove to the church, he grabbed my hand and said to me seriously, 'It's not too late, love. You don't have to do this if you don't want to.'

I'd been appalled at the idea of pulling out, angry at the suggestion I might be making a mistake. But now I see it, the door he was opening for me, the chance he was giving me to cause a scandal and break a heart; to keep a church of people waiting indefinitely if I wanted to change my mind. Did he know something that I didn't? Did Dad suspect that Isaac wouldn't be the man to keep up with me, that I'd struggle to pull him along into the adventures I needed to have, the sunlight and waves where I needed to play? But my wedding wasn't a mistake and I had no choice: I wanted Isaac then, and marrying him was the only way to have him.

I look out to the horizon. Now this wave's a beauty. It's coming right at me. I catch it just right, paddling as fast as I can to stay ahead of the crest, and then I'm coasting faster and faster, and being shot straight into the rising sun, all on my own. I'm refusing to blink because the blue and the green and the gold are all too beautiful to miss and I want to remember them forever.

~⦿

Back at the hotel entrance, tables and chairs have been set out on the seagull-splattered pavement in front, a glass windbreak erected so guests can drink their coffee and gaze at the ocean. The seat of my shorts is wet and my hair drips down my back as I find a white plastic chair in the direct sunshine. I shut my eyes and raise my face to the sun, hearing my breath deepen and slow as I relax. I have no sunscreen on but I don't care. Burn me, burn me, I think.

I pull out my phone and dial Jay's number. It will be late morning in Melbourne – he's bound to be asleep with the phone turned off. I'll try; I need to talk to him.

'Hello you!' he says as he picks up. He sounds sleepy but happy.

'Did I wake you up? I did, didn't I?'

'I left the phone on, hoping you would,' he says.

'I wanted to last night. But –'

'I can hear seagulls.'

'I'm outside,' I say. 'I just went for a swim on my own and I was catching waves too, big ones. And the sun was coming up, straight into my eyes, and I was trying not to think of sharks. I'm still dripping.' The words pour out of me because I know he's really listening, and I'm still excited from the surf.

'Brave wet girl.' I can almost hear a purr in his voice. 'I wish I could've swum with you. You're Aphrodite, reborn in the sea.' Jay loves the ocean almost as much as I do. He is a Piscean, through and through. 'Hey, when can I see you?' he asks. 'When does your plane get in?'

'Midnight, I think.'

'I don't suppose you could come straight over? Or I could pick you and Isaac up?'

'As if.' I imagine Isaac's horror if I proposed this idea. 'Anyway, I'd be pretty useless to you tonight. I'm so exhausted. Tomorrow morning?'

'Come over as early as you can. Just keep banging on my door if there's no answer.'

'Are you sure?'

'I'm sure.'

And now I'm smiling because I can't wait to see him. He feels like home.

The newspaper is still on the floor when I walk into the hotel room. It's dark and quiet and the air smells stale after the salty freshness. I rip open the drapes and slide back the balcony door to let in the light and the breeze.

Isaac moans. 'Cruel!' He rolls over, pulling a pillow onto his face.

'You're missing the day,' I say impatiently.

'Need coffee,' he croaks.

I plug in the kettle with its too-short cord and clatter the cups, relishing the way this must jangle his nerves. I make a mess with the tiny sachets of chemically dried brown granules and pure white sugar, then drip in the stupid little gulps of long-life milk — just enough to cloud up the brew but not enough to make it creamy.

'We shouldn't drink this, it's probably carcinogenic,' I say loudly as I stir the mixture, slopping the wet spoon onto the polished wooden counter beside the television. I take the coffee, along with the newspaper, and set them next to Isaac, plopping myself down on the bed beside him, pushing him roughly over with my hip to make room.

He looks up at me, bleary. 'You're so mean to me!' Then he sees my wet hair and bathers. 'Have you been out already? It's not even nine o'clock.'

'I had a run and a swim. It was gorgeous out there.'

'You're crazy, woman.'

'*You* are. You won't even touch the ocean before we leave, will you?'

'I saw it from the balcony,' he says. 'That was nice.'

I stroke the hair out of his eyes and sense the heaviness of him again, the weight of trying to make him move. I'm tired of thinking about it, tired of working away at the knot of our marriage.

'I'm having a shower,' I say, stripping off my shorts and bathers and throwing them in the corner where a fine mist of sand rains on the burgundy carpet. The maid must empty litres of sand from the vacuum cleaner every day.

'Nice arse,' Isaac says, as I walk into the bathroom.

I look back to smile at him, but he's already reading the paper.

'Don't lie around too long,' I say. 'We should go down for breakfast soon. Esther and Claudia will be here at eleven and we need to pack.'

'Yeah, yeah, yeah,' he says, and I know he'll take his own sweet time.

~♥

We're in the foyer, our suitcases leaning against our knees, watching the sliding doors for Esther and Claudia. They're half an hour late and I'm starting to worry. I can't stand waiting and I panic irrationally at the slightest sign of being stood up.

I know it's the legacy of Marcus, all those years of being in love with the boy least likely to turn up on time. All those hours I spent waiting for him to show up, or for his calls from the phone box; waiting for his car to start, or for him to wake from that deep, dead sleep of his. How horrible it was to be pitied by my friends who knew him, and would look at me sitting there, the words unsaid in their smiles: *Waiting for Marcus again, you poor little fool.*

I wonder what he's doing right now, and when I'll hear from him again. It's only a matter of time.

'Don't stress,' says Isaac, taking my hand and stilling my fingers, which are tapping against the glass table between us. 'We've still got heaps of time to get to the airport.'

He's jotting numbers down in a little black notebook with a pencil, occasionally rubbing them out with the eraser on the end, working on an equation just for fun. That used to impress me. Now I know it's as prosaic, compulsive and ultimately pointless as filling out a crossword puzzle. His long legs are stretched in front of him and his glasses have slipped to the end of his shiny nose.

I wish I could be so relaxed. I try to focus on the couples checking out at the counter. There's a chic older woman, maybe fifty-five, with bug-eye sunglasses worn on the top of her head like a tortoiseshell Alice-band. She has bobbed blonde hair and she's wearing a floaty white shirt that skims the tricky tummy and hips region. Her slim linen pants finish just above her tanned ankles. She has narrow, neat feet in gold sandals and her toenails are painted bright coral. She's standing next to her husband – I guess he's her husband, from the clumps of rings on her fingers. He's a handsome silver fox with a gold credit card, which he slides across the counter to fix up the bill. Do they still have sex, I wonder? Does he have a mistress? What would it be like to be faithful for thirty years, forty years, fifty years? For all I know, they're having a dirty, adulterous weekend. No, they look too bored and comfortable for that. And they have too much luggage.

Claudia bursts through the doors looking hot and flustered. Everyone stares over at her as she comes in, filling the space immediately. 'I'm so sorry we're late!' she shouts, oblivious. 'Esther's doing laps around the block because she doesn't want to put money in a meter, so we have to wait out the front. We slept in.'

She's wearing flowing, silky pants and an old t-shirt. Wait, are they her pyjamas?

'No problem,' says Isaac, smiling and kissing her. 'Eve was fuming, though. You know how she is about time.' He winks at me.

'Yes, I know. Poor you.' Claudia puts her head on the side sympathetically as she takes my bag from me, leading the way out.

We wait on the kerb. The sun is bright and hot, but the breeze blows up from the water with a wuthering intensity. I breathe it in deeply and say goodbye to the ocean, vowing to come back soon.

'Hurry up, Esther, I'm burning up,' says Claudia. 'I wish I had my hat.'

Then we're in the car, and as Isaac puts our bags in the boot, Esther smiles back at me over her sunnies and I can see no apology. She knows she's late and that I'm cross, but she's not going to be sorry. Bitch.

'We stayed up late,' she explains, 'watching *Trainspotting*. Claudia hadn't seen it at the movies and I wasn't going to watch it, but then I got sucked in, and afterwards we got our second wind.'

'Then we decided to make nachos,' breaks in Claudia, as she leans forward to turn up the air conditioning. 'We had to drive around to find a petrol station that was open on New Year's Day to buy corn chips. It just got later and later. Two late nights in a row for me.'

She's so proud of herself, and it makes me happy to think of the two of them getting along, watching a film, indulging in nachos and then brushing their teeth before going off to their bedrooms, with only a wall between them.

The big brick mansions with sea views and their wide open streets are flying past as we head inland. Then we're on that barren stretch of highway out to the airport, where ugly factories cling to the scrubby verge and truck fumes rise off the road and sit low, making even the finest day seem dirty. It reminds me of where I live in Melbourne, where Isaac has said we must stay. I dread going back.

~⊘

Esther and Claudia look tired and wretched as they wait for our call to board. We're sitting in the airport bar with sports channels on television screens polluting the ceiling, drawing our eyes up to the cricket even though none of us cares about it. There are overpriced drinks resting on garish beer coasters. A couple of British blokes at the bench next to us are commentating loudly, as if they want us to look over and admire them with their sunburnt flesh and ugly board shorts. We refuse to see them.

There isn't anything to say.

We're all sick of this airport. The carnival is over. The summer is still young – it's barely begun in Melbourne and probably won't even get hot until the kids go back to school in three weeks' time. But our holiday is finished. It's time for me to stop drinking wine and pack away my bathers; to go back to writing my thesis, pulling words and ideas out of the tarry muck of my lazy brain. I'll have to resume the trite, joyless rituals of the gym and the supermarket and the housework.

'So glum, chum,' says Claudia, putting an arm around me and taking another sip of her Coke. 'Won't it be nice to sleep in your own bed tonight, though?'

'I guess.'

'Before she gets into Jay's bed,' says Isaac, looking intently out the window as a jet takes off.

Silence.

'Hey, Eve, come to the loos with me,' says Esther, jumping off her bar stool. I flee with her and as the heavy door shuts behind us and we're standing in the silent ladies' room in front of the mirror, she takes my hands and looks at me hard. 'Are you going to be okay?'

'I don't know. Last night was sad. We ended up crying.'

'Because of New Year's? Or Jay? What happened?'

'I don't even know. I was coming down off the drugs and we were both tired and emotional. It feels like something's dying.'

'Listen,' she says, stroking my face and wiping a bit of smudged mascara from under my eye, 'call me tomorrow and let me know you're okay. And I'm going to come over to Melbourne and spend Easter with you, okay? So when things get bad – *if* they get bad – just remember that, so you have something to look forward to.'

'I'd love that.' Three months away, only three months. I can do that.

She pulls me in for a hug and I breathe in the warm, slightly sweaty smell of her hair and her neck as I put my face in it – she didn't have time for a shower this morning. She smells like my childhood, my home, the one I can never live in.

Out at the bar, Isaac and Claudia are hunched over her camera, fiddling with the settings.

'Hey, I've got four more photos to finish on this reel,' says Claudia, looking at us. 'Let's use them up so I can get them developed this afternoon.'

'I look like shit,' says Esther, pulling lip gloss out of her bag.

'Rubbish,' says Claudia, but it's true that we're all lacking varnish today. Nevertheless, we try each permutation of our cluster for the camera: me and Esther, cheeks jammed together like Siamese twins; me and Esther and Claudia, like the three monkeys resisting evil; Isaac and me, our arms entwined possessively across each other's bodies, as if we're honeymooners. Then Isaac flirts as he pulls us all into his embrace while a stranger clicks the final shot of us smiling madly.

Now they're calling our flight for boarding. We gather ourselves into a tight little group to the left of the departure gate. Esther hugs me so tightly I think I will break, and she whispers into my ear, 'Be strong.' Claudia kisses my cheeks, both of them, and starts to cry. Isaac wipes her tears with a finger, then kisses the finger, and she giggles.

'I'm scared – I don't want to fly,' I blurt out.

'You'll be fine,' says Esther. 'Relax.'

'Have another drink on the plane,' says Claudia. 'Have two. I wish I had a Valium to give you.'

And then I'm holding one of Claudia's hands, then one of Esther's, as Isaac pulls me away to the gate by the strap of my handbag. We slide our boarding passes across to the lipsticked guardian angels with their plastic smiles and floral scent. They slot our cards into the machine and waft us through the gate. We turn, waving and not quite ready to lose sight of the girls. They're there on tippy-toes, with their arms waving in the air.

We have to go around the corner, and all of a sudden it's just me and Isaac. We're alone in the air-locked corridor that leads down to the waiting plane. It's strangely quiet in here. The revving of the engine vibrates underfoot and the smell of kerosene is suddenly strong.

~∽

We're in our seats now, strapped into these narrow capsules, Isaac looking out the window like a child, watching the runway. Men and machines move around self-importantly with their trailers of luggage. Isaac loves it and he's humming under his breath in pleasure.

I hate it. I sit with my eyes shut, head resting back against the starched white antimacassar. I try to take deep breaths and think of other things. I rustle around in my bag for a magazine to distract me from the fact that the engines are gunning louder and we're starting to taxi down the runway. We're speeding up and I think my veins will burst with anxiety. I'm going to die, I'm going to die. I know it. I've dreamt it a thousand times – the crash, the fall, the fire and the smoke. If only I could bypass those last frantic minutes of horrified awareness, just move straight into the peace of death.

No, I don't want to die. My life's been so short and empty. There hasn't been enough of it. I want more, I want more. There has to be more.

Isaac wraps his arm through mine and twines his fingers around my own. He leans in close so that his mouth is near my ear. 'See that engine out there?'

'Mm.' I open one eye for a quick look at the wing outside the window, and then nod.

'There are four of them. And if one stops working, there's another one. And if that stops working, there's another one.'

He speaks in that calm way of his, the liturgy of science. He tells me of the laws of physics and the history of flight, and the precautions and safeguards that are taken by engineers, ground crew, pilots and flight attendants. He conjures up the statistics that do not lie. And even though I know those statistics are misleading, I don't argue because I don't want to break the spell.

I feel the earth disappear from under the wheels in that heavy, lurching moment that's the most dangerous of all: the moment when accidents happen.

But slowly, slowly, Isaac's words charm the nightmare images out of my mind. I'm clinging on to those words for dear life, just the way I'm clinging on to his hand now with my eyes tightly shut. Gusts of turbulence buffet the body of the plane as we climb higher. I dig my fingernails into his hands, but he doesn't flinch. I feel like we're a pair of survivors, so freshly wounded and shocked that we can't even bear to look down at our own damaged flesh.

But his words comfort me, though I walk through the valley of the shadow of death. I don't know if we're going to fall. I don't know if we're going to fly. Is it even possible? But we're here together in the air and when I open my eyes I see that we've pushed through the thick layer of white cloud, up, up and out, finally, into the blue. The cabin is flooded with late afternoon sunlight and the seatbelt signs are turned off. We're floating, suspended as if by faith, and we're headed towards home.

Epilogue

MELBOURNE, 2014

It's late in the afternoon. The spring sunshine is streaming through the slatted wooden blinds, and my two fat-bodied cats lie sleeping in the warmth. I calculate it's just after lunchtime in Perth – Isaac will be at work. Such irony that he lives there now, in a city he so despised twenty years ago. Does he shut the curtains, I wonder, and make his house dark all through that long heat-blasted summer?

I wonder what his house looks like.

It's been a long time since we talked, though we sometimes favourite each other's Tweets and like each other's Facebook posts. We can trace each other's lives – if we choose to – through filtered photographs and public pronouncements, and also through the gossip that travels along the Church grapevine: a vine still thick and strong, though it's broken now, in parts. It connects Isaac's parents and mine, and the cousins and friends we once shared.

Sometimes I hear from Claudia that her grandmother saw Isaac at church on Sabbath, leading the prayers and collecting the offerings. I can imagine him there, standing tall in his suit and tie at the end of each pew, smiling benevolently at the old ladies as they pass back the velvety pouch with its polished wooden handles. Maybe he helps afterwards too, to count the money, bag it and send it on to the mission-fields to continue God's work. This is how my father's wage is paid.

I need to tell Isaac about my book. He needs to know it's coming.

'Hallo, hallo!' His voice is bright and pleased. He knows it's me from caller ID.

'Hello you,' I say, and feel the warmth flowing into the line from my end, involuntary affection bubbling up at the sound of that familiar voice.

'What's up?' he asks. 'Is everything okay?'

I guess he wonders if there's been a birth or death or marriage, because those are the reasons we tend to contact each other.

'Yes, everything's good … I think,' I say tentatively. 'Remember my novel, the one I wrote about us a long time ago?'

'Yes.' Pause.

'It's going to be published. I've reworked it. As a memoir.'

'I see.'

Silence. I can feel him absorbing it. I imagine his lips pressed together as he looks out the window, wincing; or maybe he's staring at the screen on his desk, moving an icon around with his mouse, distracting himself while he gathers his words.

'Well, I suppose I should say congratulations,' he says eventually, mock-heartily.

'Thanks. It's kind of scary.' I swivel on my leather office chair, turning away from my desk so that I'm facing the mirrored wardrobe doors. I see my reflection. My hair is so red now, blazing like artificial fire in the sunlight. Evil. My eyes stare back innocently, but I wonder if I'm a monster, like every writer who's ever used their loved ones for material.

'It's what you wanted, isn't it?' he says. 'To write a book.'

'Yes, but –'

'Well, what do you want then? My blessing?'

'I don't want you to be upset.'

'Does it matter if I'm upset?' he asks. 'You'll do what you have to do, whether I like it or not. Like you always have.'

Silence.

'Sorry, that wasn't fair,' he says, gently. 'You know I'd defend to the death your right to say what you want to say, and tell the truth as you see it.'

I remember now his high principles, and the way he waved them like a flag, proclaimed them often, as if they might protect him from the messy reality of feelings. My feelings and his. The way he could never ask me to stop what I was doing, even when it hurt him, if he believed it was my right to do it. And the way I could never hear him asking in his helpless and submerged way.

Was I wilfully blind? Maybe I still am.

He sighs. 'You're a good writer, and it's an interesting story, even if it's not my version of what happened. But I have to tell you, I do feel incredibly exposed.'

'I know.' I search for something to make it better. 'You're written with love,' I say, after a while. 'And I'm the one who comes off worst – the wayward wife, the slut.'

'Stop it,' he says sternly. 'We did it together.'

'Well, you make a great character,' I say. 'A beautiful character.'

He laughs. 'Just what I always wanted to be. A *character*.'

'I'm sorry,' I say.

'It's okay. I'll live with it.' He sounds brave and weary.

'Jay doesn't mind being a character,' I say, knowing immediately that I shouldn't have mentioned Jay, but unable to stop myself.

'Of course Jay doesn't mind. He never gave a shit about anything.' It's the closest I've heard Isaac come to bitterness. 'Do you still see him, then?' he asks, as if bracing himself for an answer he'll hate.

'He was here yesterday, taking my author photo in the garden.' I remember the hours of posing and laughing; Jay pointing the camera at me, and me smiling right down into the lens, the way I always have with him because I know he really sees me. And I know he'll lose the bad ones. 'He's part of my family.'

'That's nice for you,' says Isaac. 'After everything he put you through.'

'Well, if you ever wanted me to be punished, I guess I was with Jay,' I say brightly, compressing into one sentence the painful year when I left Isaac, and Jay wasn't ready for me. I was a trembling, volatile mess, changing my mind every day about whether I was staying or leaving, a vine without a stake. No wonder Jay fell in love with somebody else. Somebody simpler. Somebody sane.

There were tears, so many tears. And sex, and trying not to have sex. And blood, when I slit my wrists because I couldn't stand it anymore. But only with a serrated kitchen knife. I wanted to be saved, and Jay drove through red lights to do it.

That was a long time ago. Something good survived the massacre and the eerie silence of two years when I couldn't see or speak to Jay. But the precious man I live with now, the father of my child, loves Jay like a brother. They share books and music and trips to the theatre, and an infuriating tendency to out-pun each other while I roll my eyes and groan. My son joins in now, and I love looking at the three of them when we eat at our favourite Vietnamese restaurant in Footscray, greedy boys wolfing down spring rolls.

'I never wanted you to be punished,' says Isaac kindly. 'But I don't really need that part of my life out in the open.'

'Sorry,' I say again, and I know how ineffectual it sounds.

'It's just that I lead a very different life now. I'm quite conservative, you know. Traditional.'

'I know you go to church,' I say. 'But tell me, honestly …' I'm conspiratorial now, wanting him to confess secrets. 'Do you really believe it all?'

'I do,' he says, as if it's a vow.

'Every bit of it?' I'm incredulous. 'Six days of creation? The Cross? The imminent Second Coming of Christ?'

'I do,' he says again.

'You believe you're going to Heaven in the sky after the Resurrection? And that Jesus is coming in the clouds?' It sounds so ridiculous to me now, as I know it does to my son when I try to tell him what his grandparents believe, and he says, as he slurps his chocolate milkshake, 'But, Mum, we just go back to the dirt when we die and that's okay. It's a part of life. Deal with it.'

Sometimes I wonder if my boy's pragmatism will hold up to real tragedy, and I suspect that his worldview lacks the poetry and magic of the one I grew up with. But it's also missing the fear, and the guilt and the worry about Last Days persecution. He loves to snorkel, my boy, a small human fish so at home in the garden under the sea, where he swims in a rainbow school with Esther's three children and Claudia's two when we holiday together. He wonders and worries if his own children will get to see the Great Barrier Reef before it's gone. But he seems so happy and so free. Or is that wishful thinking?

'Yes, I believe all of it,' says Isaac simply.

'Wow.' I'm stunned. He's a scientist, a rationalist, a trained logician. And yet I remember again how common-sense it all seemed when we were taught the Bible with our mothers' milk.

'I don't think I ever really lost faith,' he says, 'the way you did.'

~⊙

I look over to the spare bed where photos are strewn across the patchwork coverlet. After leaving my old albums to gather dust for decades in a high cupboard, I've dragged them out, searching for clues as I finish the book. There are so many pictures of my son when he was a baby. I still made albums then, before we went digital. One of my favourites shows him ten months old, his big round head still fluffy with down. With one of his chubby hands he's pulling on Marcus' dreadlocks. I remember that visit when a strange and perfect circle felt completed. They're both sucking their thumbs and laughing at the camera.

But it's earlier albums that I needed for this project.

'I've been looking at pictures of us this week,' I say to Isaac. 'God, you were beautiful.'

'Heh, really? I'm not anymore,' he says gruffly.

'But we were so young!' I glance at a photo of the two of us, haloed in winter sunshine in some ferny grove in the Dandenongs. It's a blurry, overexposed snap, taken by Esther on one of her visits. Isaac is kissing me, my head thrown back theatrically for effect. I'm wearing a skivvy and my hair is hanging down to my waist. I must have been twenty-two then, the year before I cut it into a bob. His own hair is long and free and dark. We look like hippies.

'We were such children,' I say. 'Babies. We didn't know anything, and we wanted to try things.'

'We certainly did that.'

'But we really loved each other,' I say.

'Yes, we really did.'

My eyes fill with tears, the way they always do when I think too much about Isaac and me and how we failed. How I failed, particularly, to honour my promises: *Till death do us part. Forsaking all others.* My failure is so huge and momentous that I'll never wear a wedding ring or make a marriage vow again, no matter how entwined my fate may be with another. The man I've loved these past sixteen years – another scientist with a fine, brilliant mind and a wise heart (so much like Isaac in some ways, yet so different because his own religion is nature) – has his own divorce story and a rebel's distaste for bourgeois convention. His love for me is elastic and wholehearted. And he understands that for me to marry again would feel dishonest, would require a clean slate I can never allow myself. Because I know what I'm capable of.

I want to cry. This is why Isaac and I stopped seeing each other, several years after the separation – it just made me cry every time I saw his face. Too many embarrassing scenes in cafes. Sadness that had no point and no resolution.

'Hey,' I say, pulling myself up straight, 'I need to go and do the school pickup.'

'How is he, your boy?' Isaac asks.

'He's golden.' I smile at the thought of him. 'How's yours?'

'Golden too,' says Isaac, laughing. 'He never stops talking now.'

'I bet he's like you. Is he like you?' I try to picture the child whose mother I've never met.

'Poor little critter,' says Isaac fondly.

'Lucky creature. He'll be amazing.'

Isaac laughs at my flattery. 'Stop it!'

'Hey, I'm going to be late,' I say, looking at the clock on my computer screen and pulling on my boots.

'Go, go,' Isaac says. 'Let's talk soon, though, okay? More about the book. I need to read it again.'

'Of course, if you want to. And thank you for not hating me too much for doing it.'

'As if I could.'

~ৎ

I'm driving as fast as I dare now, racing the clock to my son's school. I'm heading west, straight into the glare. The fumes from the trucks and the dust from the factories filter it all into gold and orange, with apricot clouds so beautiful against the blue that I think again how lucky I am to live in Melbourne's dirty inner west, where the skies seem higher and the people still full of frontier hopes.

Some days are black, some years are bad, and I can see the lines on my face now, though I try not to mind them. Sometimes I'm still hungry and sometimes I want more, and that's who I am. I don't know if I'm going to fall and I don't know if I'm going to fly, but right now I feel alive, so alive, balanced on white lines heading to infinity.